The No-Fear Entrepreneur

Good Words About The *No-Fear* Entrepreneur

Freedom from fear is one of the sweetest liberties in life, and yet sometimes this freedom can be elusive. For those desiring to launch a new business, reach a particular career goal, or complete a major project, like writing a book, fear of failure—or even of success—can be so daunting it can actually keep you from fulfilling your dreams. In his new book, *The No-Fear Entrepreneur* John Thurman gives practical keys to help those who are struggling to identify their fears, acknowledge them, and find a way to freedom. John completes the journey by giving a list of action steps that will help entrepreneurs face and overcome any fear, freeing you to push through to success.

Craig von Buseck, Author, Speaker, Chaplain

FEAR? I've been a leader in direct sales for almost 27 years and that is one word that I've never struggled with until now. As things are changing in the business-sales world at such a rapid pace, I've found myself getting paralyzed and missing opportunities due to fear. In John Thurman's book, *The No-Fear Entrepreneur*, he identifies the thought process and the causes and effects of fear. This book, by far, has the most practical solutions to help us unlock and conquer our most common fears. Don and I have known John for more than twenty-five years, and he brings such a unique perspective as both a mental health professional and entrepreneur. I highly recommend this book!

Tandy Flynn, 7 Diamond Designer with Premier Designs

Every day, I work with businesses and ministries that are stuck. They are stuck not because of a lack of finances, a lack of customers, or a lack of talent, but stuck in paralyzing fear of the "but what ifs." This fear is keeping brilliant people not only stuck, but falling further and further behind.

In his book *The No-Fear Entrepreneur*, John Thurman gets to the root of that fear for entrepreneurs and fights it with research, logic, and inspiring stories of the people who have recognized the fear and finally, done something about it. If you're stuck, this is the book to get you moving forward.

Kathi Lipp, Bestselling Author and Founder of CommunicatorAcademy.com

Fear is something we all face. How do we handle an emotion we cannot see? Fear can paralyze us, or we can use it to move forward in a positive way as we reach our next goals. John Thurman confronts and explains how the emotion of fear can make us, break us, or mold us. Can this help you? Don't be fearful in finding out. Start reading right away—I dare you!!

Greg Terrell, Executive Director, Premier Designs Jewelry since 1987

John Thurman's book, *The No-Fear Entrepreneur* was so good that I was afraid to put it down for fear I would miss out on something I needed to know in order to succeed in my life and business. Seriously, this book was completely relevant and targeted specifically to the unique needs and struggles I have every day. It is a must read for any type of business, but especially for those in network marketing. It is filled with practical and invaluable insights from a biblical and psychological perspective.

Gayle Foster, Diamond Executive Director, Premier Designs

Fear is the monster hiding under the bed that we really don't want to face. But John Thurman tosses the covers back and shines the flashlight of truth into the darkest corners. In that light, fear is reduced to what it is: a manageable, normal emotion. By giving biblical perspective and simple strategies, along with open honesty about his own struggles, he helped me get a grip on my own fear. Even I didn't know how much I needed to read this book!

Katherine Graves, Strong Foundation Ministries

The No-Fear Entrepreneur offers you the opportunity to turn your fear into faith and power. The practical steps offered, the quotes and stories, as well as John's wealth of wisdom, is worth remembering for a lifetime. This is one of those books that will be referred to again and again as a resource for personal enrichment as well as encouraging others to get a grip on fear.

Doreen Hanna, International Speaker & Author, Founder & President of Treasured Celebrations

John Thurman has written an engaging book for anyone who has ever struggled with fear. And don't we all struggle with that at some point? Whether it's fear of failure or fear of success, this book is for everyone.

Jennifer Munneke-Keller, 5 Diamond Designer, Premier Designs

Whether you are working to build a championship team or a successful network marketing business, you must "get a grip on fear." In his book, *The No-Fear Entrepreneur,* John Thurman details exactly what fear is, how it works to stifle growth when it is in control, and, most importantly, how to overcome and use it to build success. A great way to get a grip on fear is to get a grip on John's book.

Coach Barry Phal, Ohio Basketball Hall of Fame—2012

What a terrific, positive, inspiring book! Packed with moving stories, challenging perspectives, and stimulating Bible studies, *The No-Fear Entrepreneur* will appeal to entrepreneurs (and their long-suffering spouses). Perhaps not all, but certainly those, like me, who struggle against fear and think ourselves lacking some brain cells or a necessary faith switch. Thurman says, no, we're very normal, and he offers us some tips to plow through and find success. Anyone strong enough to admit that their fears often immobilize them from reaching the success they desire will read this book without stopping. Thurman's style is positive, honest, assertive, faithful to biblical teaching, and includes a healthy dose of pragmatic science. As both a therapist and an entrepreneur, Thurman speaks as an authority. He helps his readers understand the roots of those nagging, hated, irrational fears. He goes on to offer simple, satisfying studies and exercises to get past the halting fears and make that next call, submit that next proposal, or get back up one more time, which is often the key to achievement, don't you agree? If you're entrepreneurial and simply investigating Christianity, this book offers some deep points to consider. The idea that God is for you, and wants you to overcome the negative aspects of fear, may be just the refreshing insight you seek. Believer or skeptic, I highly recommend John Thurman's *The No-Fear Entrepreneur.*

Jack M. Allen, PhD, Dynamic Coaching, Austin

The No-Fear Entrepreneur

John H. Thurman Jr.

BVB

Bold Vision Books
PO Box 2011
Friendswood, Texas 77549

Table of Contents

Foreword

With my wife Angie, I have been honored to be involved with a wonderful direct service/sales company, Premier Designs Jewelry, for more than twenty years. In this journey we have had our share of ups and downs, of great seasons, and lack-luster seasons. In all of that time, several key factors have kept us going.

Faith in God. Faith in ourselves. Friends. Caring, encouraging leaders. And our commitment to personal goals and dreams.

Angie and I believe that one of the reasons America is such a great country is our free enterprise system, which gives everyone an opportunity to build a business and pursue their dreams. No matter what in individual's background, ethnicity, or creed, in America, individuals can have a dream of owning their own business and build it, with minimal government control. In that system, there are no guarantees, no government bailout, and no ceiling on what a person can do.

Every day, new entrepreneurs enter the marketplace with new concepts, ideas, and services, including those who establish home-based businesses with the hope of having enriching their families, pay bills, or increasing their leisure income.

A Word about Biblical Entrepreneurship and Success

What comes to your mind when you hear the word entrepreneur? For many people, it's the image of someone who is always hustling, trying to whatever they can to turn a buck.

Personally, I like the idea that an entrepreneur is a someone who habitually creates and innovates to build something of value around perceived opportunity.

The woman spoken of in Proverbs 31 was such a person. When we study her, we see that as a woman made in God's image, she was a profitable, creative business woman, whose business increased and profited others.

It's my personal belief that God wants us to succeed in our endeavors, but not always in the traditional sense of money, power, and prestige.

Here is something to think about as we begin to get into the meat of this book.

God wants us to operate as one who is blessed and wishes to share his blessings with others. After all, He owns it all. Being blessed to be a blessing to others sets in motion God's faith-gift increase. To create, bring increase, and multiply are key parts of God's very nature. Being created *imageo Deo*, in His image, means that we are blessed to do the same. These same dynamics are at the heart of entrepreneurship.

Recently I was having a lively conversation with a fellow therapist, who was also working with his wife in a direct service/sales organization. We were having a discussion about people who are either relatively new in such a business or are merely looking at the opportunity and quickly become overwhelmed with fear. This book is a direct result of that conversation. Over the years I have had hundreds of conversations with men and women who have struggled with fear. I admit that I had to deal with fear and a type of arrogant pride when my wife I and started our journey in the direct service/sales business.

As a therapist, I wanted to have a deeper understanding of what the common fears were and develop practical tools budding entrepreneurs could use to more effectively reach their success goals.

On the subject of fear, Pastor Andy Stanley says, "The human race is notorious for being afraid of the wrong things. The trail of history is littered with discarded fears that once erroneously controlled mankind's destiny."

Fear is probably the biggest boogeyman in the direct sales profession.

This being the case, I enlisted the aid of other researchers and mental health friends to help me design a survey to understand the types of fears that Premier Design Jewelry consultants face. Of 1500 who were surveyed, 236 responded. The survey was a blind survey, in that the research team had no idea of the respondents' identities. This survey was conducted July 7th through the 14th , 2015 via Survey Monkey.

This resource is designed to share what I learned and give you proven, practical tools to deal with entrepreneurial fear and experience renewed joy and intentionality.

Here are the details of the survey.

Total respondents 236.

Women respondents	226
Male respondents	10

Age Spread

18-24	1.7%
25-34	22.98%
35-44	29.39%
45-54	28.94%
55-64	14.89%
65-74	1.70%
75 +	.43%

Highest level of school completed

High School	8.7%
Some College	22.88%
Two - year College Degree	16.10 %
Four - year degree	33.47%
Graduate–level degree	18.64%
None of the above	.21%

Marital Status

Married	81.36%
Widowed	1.69%
Divorced	8.47%
Separated	.85%

In a domestic partnership	1.27%
Single, but cohabitating	2.54%
Single, never married	3.81%

Six common Fears that Premier Jewelers Face.

	Never	Sometimes	Often	Always
1. Fear of Rejection (94.85)	5.15%	37.77%	31.76%	25.32%
2. Fear of Failure (92.74)	7.26%	37.61%	34.62%	20.51%
3. Fear of Criticism (82.98)	17.02%	54.89%	20.43%	7.66%
4. Fear of Decision Making (74.24)	25.75%	50.21%	19.31%	4.72%
5. Fear of Public Speaking (64.94)	36.05%	39.91%	14.59%	9.44%
6. Fear of Responsibility (64.71)	35.90%	40.60%	14.96%	8.55%

What have you done to help with your fear?

	Never	Sometimes	Often	Always
Pray	9%	13.45%	40.36%	45.29%
Read motivational books	5.22%	46.52%	37.39%	10.87%
Attend training	1.29%	17.60%	29.18%	51.93%

Talk with Up/Cross line				
	4.35%	37.83%	35.66%	22.17%
Do what I need to do	3.04%	35.22%	39.57%	22.17%
Hire a coach	87.88%	8.66%	1.30%	2.16%

Talk with Up/Cross line				
	4.35%	37.83%	35.66%	22.17%
Do what I need to do	3.04%	35.22%	39.57%	22.17%
Hire a coach	87.88%	8.66%	1.30%	2.16%

Introduction

Congratulations on having the courage to purchase this book. I know from personal experience that starting any enterprise, especially a new business or ministry, can be a challenging task on a deeply personal level. I am proud you have taken the challenge and want to push through the fear.

I'd like to begin with personal disclosure. Just like you, I have faced my own challenges with the boogeyman called fear during different phases and stages of my life. It's that primal, negative, gut-wrenching feeling that has, at times, impaired my decision-making abilities. And because I did not address that fear, but tried to pretend it was not there, my method of handling the fear produced a negative impact on me, my marriage, and our family. Thankfully, we are the on the other side of that experience now.

As I worked on this project, frankly, some of those old memories of failures and hesitations raised their ugly, ghoulish heads and attempted to distract me. So why am I telling you this?

One of the rewards of accumulating close to 40,000 hours of working with individuals and couples is that, while helping others, a smart counselor must monitor their own stuff. While my goal is to provide proven, faith-friendly principles with a biblical perspective, on a deeper level this is personal. I know what it is like to wake up at three in the morning with my mind racing over some negative comment someone made about me, my idea, my dream.

My heartfelt prayer is that you will not only learn and implement some of these principles concerning how to get a grip on fear, but that the truths of the Scripture will richly dwell in your heart and head and provide you hope, insight, and guts. More than that, I want you to know God will bless you, strengthen you, and encourage you as you lean into the fear that has been holding you back for so long.

Before we jump in, please take a moment to read this ancient prayer called the *Breastplate of St. Patrick*.

Steven James, a prolific Christian fiction writer, quoted the prayer verbatim at the beginning of his class at the Class Seminars Writer's Conference a few years ago. I'd never heard it before, and it stuck with me. *St. Patrick's Breastplate* is a traditional prayer attributed to one of Ireland's most beloved patron saints. According to tradition, St. Patrick wrote it in 433 A.D. for divine protection before successfully converting the Irish King Laoghaire and his subjects from paganism to Christianity. (The term *breastplate* refers to a piece of armor worn in battle.)

More recent scholarship suggests its author was anonymous. In any case, this prayer certainly reflects the spirit with which St. Patrick brought our faith to Ireland! *St. Patrick's Breastplate*, also known as *The Lorica of Saint Patrick,* was famous enough to inspire a hymn based on this text as well. (This prayer has also been called *The Cry of the Deer*.)[1] This is a very abbreviated version of the prayer:

I arise today.
Through a mighty strength,
the invocation of the Trinity,
Through belief in the Threeness,
Through confession of the Oneness
of the Creator of creation.

When St. Paul referred to putting on the "Armor of God" in his letter to the Ephesians (6:11) to fight sin and evil inclinations, he could have been thinking of prayers just like this one! We may not wear combat gear in our daily lives, but St. Patrick's Breastplate can function as spiritual armor for protection against spiritual adversity.

With this fresh insight into the ancient prayer, let's transition into its practical application.

Did you know that there are common themes when it comes to failing in a network marketing business or any other endeavor? Here is a partial list why some entrepreneurs crash and burn. The following is adapted from *7 Reasons Why Most Entrepreneurs Fail As Much As They Succeed*, by Tito Philips.[2]

"Survival Driven" (Seeking Money Before Adding Value)

Being driven by survival is a major reason why some entrepreneurs fail. If your primary motivation is money and to acquire wealth rather than to create and increase the value to people's lives through a product, service, or an idea, then you have gotten off to a poor start. If this is your sole goal in being in business, I would suggest you do some important soul searching. When you seek to add value, it helps keep your moral compass pointing in the right direction. The purpose of owning your own business should not only focus on the accumulation of wealth but the creation of value-added products and services that will help make the world a better place for all. *Wealth is a result of consistently providing solutions to the problems of humanity.*

Inadequate Knowledge (Low Business Knowledge)

Dwight Bain is a friend of mine who has an impactful business coaching company. He and I traveled together for a speaking engagement, and while we stopped for a meal, he and I talked about the power of being a life-long learner. We discussed a recent study that indicated only 50% of Americans read a book after graduating. After a few minutes of sharing, Dwight dropped this beautiful quote, "All leaders are readers."

One of the positive things most reputable network marketing companies offer is training. The companies that, in my opinion, are truly legitimate provide training and additional learning opportunities to increase business knowledge. So, to have more means you have to do more and to do more means you need to keep learning more.

How do you find out more? By consistently focusing on personal development and self-improvement through books, blogs, magazines, webinars, training meetings and other self-directed growth. You might also consider hiring a business coach to help you move to your next level.

Lack of Focus (A Jack of All Trades, Mastering None)

Albert Einstein said, "Genius is the ability to focus on one particular thing for a long time without losing concentration."

So many network marketers fail to build their business because they are trying to do too much. While many people tell me they are multi-taskers, the clinical research suggests the opposite. As a business person, your success or failure will be a direct result of how well you maximize your strengths. Your strengths are those activities you naturally enjoy doing and would do them for free your entire life if necessary. This is how every great entrepreneur in history made their success: doing what they love and loving what they do.

If you have ever wanted to identify and understand how to live and lead with your strengths, I can help you out. I offer a package where we use time-tested instruments and my experience as a business coach to help you identify, understand, and exploit your strengths. Go to www.johnthurman.net to learn more information.

> Here is your assignment today, look at what you are doing that is not a strength area, then see if there is a way to get someone else to do it. You might find a child, a student, a relative, or a stay at home mom who could help out on a very part-time basis.

Fear of Failure (Risk Averse)

Feeding the fear is another reason entrepreneurs fail in business. Entrepreneurship is all about learning how to unleash your passion and creativity to do something you care about. It doesn't matter whether what you have in mind to create is in demand or generally acceptable. What is important is that it matters enough to you that you are willing to do whatever it takes to make your idea become a reality.

This resource, designed for you, will help you look fear in the eye and push through it. Don't allow the fear of failure to capture you. It will only lead to regret. Instead, lean into it, find some friends to take the journey with you, and exercise your faith.

Lack of Vision (Shortsightedness)

Proverbs 29:18 (KJV) says, "Where there is no vision, the people perish." Many entrepreneurs fail because of a lack of vision or dream; a failure to see themselves months or years down the road in their business. The key to overcoming a lack of vision is to ask the question consistently: "What can we start doing today to meet the needs of tomorrow?" Failure to have this in your mind is one reason why many network marketers fail. So what is your vision for your business? Become debt free, spend more time with your family, travel, give more to ministries, help people?

> From time to time, you need to review your personal vision. It will help you. I believe God plants those visions and dreams in our hearts, and as we pursue Him and work our business, our vision will increase as will our business.

Poor Money Management (Extravagance)

Being in business for yourself means you will sometimes have dramatic ups and downs in your cash flow. Being frugal, having a budget and living within it is a requirement for you if you hope to become successful. Even Jesus talked about this: "If you are faithful in little things, you will be faithful in large ones." Luke 16:10 NLT

One way to do this is to investigate financial management systems and to classify your expenses and income. I like Dave Ramsey's guidelines because they are written for non-accounting types like me.

As a word of caution, as your business begins to grow and produces income, do not become one of those who starts showing off the success of their business by buying additional symbols of wealth. Place yourself on a salary, pay your taxes on time, and find ways to redeploy your assets for a rainy-day-fund and future business expenses.

I Can Do Well By Myself (Insecurity)

I know you have heard there is no "I" in Team. There is a limit to what one person can do by themselves, thus the need for teamwork.

"A person standing alone can be attacked and defeated, but two can stand back-to-back and conquer. Three are even better, for a triple-braided cord is not easily broken." Ecclesiastes 4:12 NLT

Recently, I was on a short-term deployment to the Democratic Republic of Congo. While there I was unable to access my company email, which was critical. I was halfway around the world from my IT support, 8185 miles, as the crow flies. I was finally able to contact my IT team. Over the next few hours, with a six-hour time difference, they were able to get me reconnected. I was our company representative on the ground, but the fact that I had a supervisor and huge support team behind me made the mission a success.

It is so important for you to realize you are not alone. Whatever it is you have in your mind to create is not entirely yours to dominate. You are only a vessel through which an idea, service, or product is being launched.

Here is a lesson I learned the hard way. One of the reasons I was a Lone Ranger in my younger days was that I had some underlying insecurity. I felt that to be a man, I had to get it right. Every time. As I became older, I began to realize that nearly all men feel like they are "posers." Once I jumped over that roadblock, I found friends who were in the same boat.

In thinking about writing this book, I wanted it to be a resource, not based on clinical data points but based on life experience, validated by research.

Chapter One
A Primer on Fear

Too many of us are not living our dreams
because we are living our fears.[3]
~Les Brown

*F*ear serves one—and only one—purpose: to keep you alive. In its most basic, primal form, it is nothing more than a survival response. Fear can be a good thing. It is a profound biological instinct that can prevent us from doing crazy things that could kill us. For example, if you are working in your back yard and see a snake slithering into hedges next to your house—well, let's put it this way—I doubt you are feeling peaceful and calm.

Several years ago, Angie and I took our Jeep up to Ouray, Colorado to do some 4-wheeling. It was summer time, so we drove with the top and doors off. As we made our way up the Million Dollar Highway out of Durango, it became apparent that this trip was going to be a bit of a process. When Angie saw how narrow the road could be and that there were no rails . . . you get the picture. There is something dynamic when you are twelve inches away from a 1,000 foot drop-off.

With both the snake and the drive, this is rational fear.

Fear can produce positive energy that moves us forward, help us make a life change, and gives us new perspective. Unfortunately, while fear can protect us from pain and harm, fear is not always rational and healthy.

God didn't create us to live our lives in fear. He created us to live with power, love, and a sound mind, as in courage.

I love the way the Amplified Bible states 2 Timothy 1:7, "For God did not give us a spirit of timidity (of cowardice, craven and clinging, but [He has given us a spirit] of power and love and well-balanced mind and discipline and self-control."

Let's look at what fear does to us and in us:

First, irrational fear is a very primal, gut function. It is a basic low-level brain function. While fear can become disarming and lead to self-inflicted sabotage, it can be overcome. When we take time to think through our fears, we usually discover that those concerns are rooted in irrational thoughts.

Second, fear can make us cowards. We humans tend to frame our fears in ways that soothe our egos. You and I will say something like, "I am prudent and cautious." We might even say, "I am a little nervous." Or we say, "It's not that important."

Here is a huge life tip:

If you want to start overcoming those irrational fears that keep you bound, you are going to have to call it what it is.

Instead of saying, "I am not doing this because it makes me nervous," try saying, "I am not going to do this because I am a coward, and I am scared spitless." You will be amazed when you tell yourself the truth—aloud. That is the beginning of calling it what it is. Trust me—this is a starting point.

Third, fear steals our integrity. It makes us hypocritical. Simply stated, integrity means acting in a way wholly congruent with our values and beliefs. When we want to do something and believe it is the correct thing to do, but we fail to do it because of fear, we violate our core values. Living a "True North" life means living in alignment with our principles.

The first time I heard the term "True North" was while I was in the Army. It is a term used in map and compass training which differentiates the True North from Magnetic North difference on a topographical map. Steven Covey borrowed this term and turned it into a metaphor about our bottom line personal ethics—the line we are *unwilling* to cross based on those ethics. Therefore, when you and I are faced, as we often are in this difficult life, with the question of what direction to take, we need to refer to our true north for direction. Metaphorically: Do I "cross" my personal line? (Lie, cheat, steal, be disloyal to a loved one, hit or be abusive physically or verbally, etc.). Never lose sight of your true north.

Fourth, fear leaves lament and regret in its wake. You and I have made, and will continue to make, missteps and mistakes. The key is: Will we repeat the same screw ups again and again or will we learn from them and make the necessary adjustments to change the outcome? If you and I allow fear to keep us from seizing an opportunity when it comes our way, then that is nobody's fault but our own. Instead, we can trust that when the Lord brings us an opportunity, He will give us what we need to move towards it. But we have to get out of the boat.

Fifth, when we give in to fear, we give up control; we step away from the steering wheel, which could be deadly. You see—the Lord has given us life and choices. While He will guide us, He will not do the work for us. When we are ruled by fear, we abdicate our responsibility. That is not a good thing. You are the only one responsible for your life, no one else. At the end of this race, you and I will give an account. I want to hear Jesus say, "Well done, good and faithful servant." Matthew 25:23 NLT

Sixth, fear stifles personal growth. There seems to be a universal principle in nature: You are either getting better—ripening, or you are ripe and ready to meet your full potential, or you are rotting.

Growing up in the South, (before child labor laws tightened up), I worked as a field hand in the Miami Valley Peach Orchard in Fort Valley, Georgia. Early in the morning, I would go out with the pickers as they picked their half-bushel bags and dumped them into boxes. Each time they put the peaches in the box, they received a ticket which could later be turned in for cash. The key was to pick them just before they became ripe so they could be shipped fresh. Those peaches were getting better—ripening.

After the first picking, we would go back and pick a few ripe peaches and eat them. Mrs. Mullis owned the Fort Valley Dairy Queen, and in the summer, she would gather the peaches that were too ripe to ship and take them to her store. For a few weeks, you could order a fresh peach-vanilla shake. If a person could taste gold, she captured it. The peaches we ate and the peaches in the shakes were just right—ready to reach full potential.

My second year in the peach business, I worked for Wilson's Packing Shed. This is where the peaches were brought in from the field and prepared for shipping. In that process, there were two reasons peaches were culled. The first was due to imperfections. The second was because they were overripe. Have you ever smelled rotting fruit? Pretty nasty. Well, imagine 20 to 30 bushels of overripe and rotting peaches in the Middle Georgia heat and humidity. Thankfully, every day of so, that nastiness was removed. Those peaches were rotting.

Like peaches, there is a time when we are ripening. There is also a time when things are ready for picking. Unfortunately, rotting is also possible. Over time, fear may cause spoilage for us.

Make it your goal to be a little bit better tomorrow than you were today. I do believe that is part of God's will for your life.

How to Overcome Your Fears

"Many of our fears are tissue-paper-thin, and a single courageous step would carry us clear through them," Brendan Francis.

Here are some steps I adapted from *The Art of Manliness: 29 Days to a Better Man: Conquer Fear.*[4]

Change Your Perspective On Fear

Fear is only negative if you think it is. Fear is a natural process that if left unchecked will cause us to live timid, restricted lives. Truthfully, in life there is zero growth without risk. Instead of pushing back fear as an all-consuming, nerve-racking experience, see it as an adventure, a journey that will take you out of your comfort zone and into a whole new life and bring a sense of joy and adventure. If you have ever conquered a fear, you know it can be exhilarating. So why don't you try and scare yourself just a little today? You might like the outcome.

Adjust Your Perspective On Risk

The honest taproot for many of our fears is the fear of trying something and failing. *What if I get rejected? What if I fail?* Well, you could, but you will never know until you try. If you don't take the risk, you will never know, and you are guaranteed to fail.

This might be uncomfortable for you, but my mission is to challenge you. In making such a decision, you are leaving out the possible long-term risk, a risk that could be far greater than a risk to your ego. The long-term risk is the danger of living an entirely average life. The risk is looking back on your life in 10, 20, or 30 years and feeling your stomach turn with regret and remorse.

The primary reason we miss opportunities God sends our way is fear. It is sad to say that when you miss a chance because of your fear, you will never get that moment back again.

Maybe it is time for you to update your risk criteria.

Act with Courage

Teddy Roosevelt put it this way: *"There were all kinds of things of which I was afraid of at first, ranging from grizzly bears to 'mean' horses and gunfighters; but by acting as if I was not afraid I gradually ceased to be scared."* [5]

Think about some of the men and women of the Bible who acted courageously: Ruth, Esther, Mary, the Mother of Jesus, Gideon, David. And how about other historical figures?

SFC Leigh Ann Hester, Silver Star, American Hero.

I doubt you have heard of this hero. Sergeant now Sergeant First Class Leigh Ann Hester was the first female to win the Silver Star in the Iraq War. This was later upgraded to the Distinguished Service Cross. Here is an excerpt from the citation:

> After insurgents hit the convoy with a barrage of fire from machine guns, AK-47 assault rifles and rocket-propelled grenades, Hester "maneuvered her team through the kill zone into a flanking position where she assaulted a trench line with grenades and M203 rounds," according to the Army citation accompanying the Silver Star.
>
> "She then cleared two trenches with her squad leader where she engaged and eliminated three AIF [anti-Iraqi forces] with her M4 rifle. Her actions saved the lives of numerous convoy members," the citation stated.

She was deployed with the Virginia National Guard, where she still serves.[6]

Here are other, more well-known people who overcame fear and became world renown in their field:

Stevie Wonder, Singer.

Stevie Wonder has received 22 Grammy awards over his 51-year music career—the most Grammy awards ever received by a single male recording artist. As you probably know, Stevie Wonder has been blind since birth, but that hasn't stopped him from releasing more than 30 number one hits and being one of the greatest performers who has ever lived. At the same time, he also spearheaded many political campaigns and became an American cultural icon. He has fathered seven children, including the daughter who inspired the uplifting hit, "Isn't She Lovely," and will go down as one of the most influential music icons of all time.[7]

Richard Branson, CEO.

Richard Branson is the fourth-richest person in the United Kingdom. He owns the Virgin group of brands, including a record label, an airline, and the mobile phone company. Branson also owns an island in the Caribbean. As a child, though, he performed poorly on tests in school and struggled with dyslexia. Teachers and authority figures assumed he wouldn't go very far, but Branson defied the odds, and attributes his success to his people skills—proving street smarts can take you far.[8]

Colbie Caillat, Singer.

This artist is one of my personal favorites. I enjoy her style, attitude, and lyrics. She is a two-time Grammy winner with over six million albums and 10 million single sales to her credit. Also, she was a two-time loser on [the television show] American Idol.[9]

Reflecting back, she said, "I was shy, I was nervous. I didn't look the greatest. I wasn't ready for it. I was glad when I auditioned, and they said 'no.'"

Buzz Aldrin, Astronaut, Second Man on the Moon.

Buzz Aldrin rose through the ranks of the United States Air Force and eventually became the second man to step foot on the surface of the moon. However, his return to Earth was marred by a slew of personal problems—primarily a struggle with both depression and alcoholism. After a long battle that would truly test his strength, courage, and self-motivation, he recognized and sought treatment for both of his illnesses and has since become an outspoken supporter of space exploration. He has even received a star on the Hollywood Walk of Fame. His legacy also inspired the name of beloved cartoon character Buzz Lightyear. His personal troubles had the potential to overshadow his professional achievements, but Buzz Aldrin knew he needed help—and today he's doing better than ever.[10]

Kill Fear With Faith-Filled, Logical Thought Processes

Fear is usually a function of lack of confidence and low self-esteem. Many people are afraid because they think they will fail. But if they do it anyway—if they try to overcome their fear instead of letting their fear limit them—they find they *can* do it. Fear should not keep us from working.

> *The Lord is on my side; I will not fear;*
> *What can mere man do to me?* Psalm 118:6 (NKJV)

Think on this as we begin the freedom-from-fear journey together. Fear receives way too much airplay. Fear is the big bad boogeyman that grows by negative, contemplative thoughts that are re-runs of painful past events.

Fear is primarily mismanagement of our mental capacities.

As we move into this potentially life-changing material, let me share five factors that, if used, will expedite your abilities to push back fear:

1. Faith. The belief that God is on your side, and that He does not make any junk. Faith that He who started a good work in you will fulfill it. Faith that God is a mighty God of second chances. As a growing, sometimes struggling Christ follower I sometimes waver at this point. In my head, I know the truth, but sometimes my heart is resistant to trust.

2. The support of real friends. Friends who will both love and challenge you. Friends who will hold you accountable. We live in a unique time in history. On the one hand, we have more connectivity to each other than at any time prior, thanks to smart devices and social media. On the other hand, more people are struggling to connect with face to face relationships. Here is a prophetic word from Albert Einstein: "I fear the day that technology will surpass our human interaction. The world will have a generation of idiots." Next time you are out for dinner, take a moment to observe how many people are more engaged with their devices than with each other. Leonard Sweet, a Methodist theologian, shared an interesting comment on his Facebook page recently: "Those born after 1985 have no memory of life before the Internet. Those born before 1985 are the last remnants who have memories of living on both sides of the digital divide."[11]

I love technology; it is a big part of how I do my private counseling and consulting business. But research tells us that one of the most cost-effective ways to overcome fear is to connect directly with family and friends.

3. Time. You didn't get this way overnight, and you will not be done with it within the next three weeks. The good news is that you have started the journey by picking up this resource.

A good friend of mine who is a pastor of a growing, dynamic church gave an excellent illustration of this principle. Farmers and gardeners understand time. When they plant corn, they have a series of things that have to happen in a certain order. First, they have to prepare the soil. Then plant the seeds in a place where they will receive full sun. If the ground conditions, weather, and plant care all work together, the farmer or gardener will have corn in 60-100 days, depending on the variety.

After those initial steps, if farmers let nature take its course, they will reap a harvest. My pastor friend said, "People, we need to remember this! When dealing with life issues, many want an immediate answer and become disappointed God doesn't do something immediately.

4. Doing What You can. May I give you a word of advice? Pray about the issue. Then do your part to make the changes."

Let's look at the miracle of Jesus feeding the 5000.

> Late in the afternoon the Twelve disciples came to him and said, Send the crowds away to the nearby villages and farms so they can find food and lodging for the night. There is nothing to eat here in this remote place."
>
> But Jesus said, "You feed them." "We have only five loaves of bread and two fish," they answered. "Or are you expecting us to go and buy enough food for this whole crowd?" For there were about 5,000 men there. Jesus replied, "Tell them to sit down in groups of about fifty each." So the people all sat down. Jesus took the five loaves and two fish, looked up toward heaven, and blessed them. Then, breaking the loaves into pieces, he kept giving the bread and fish to the disciples so they could distribute it to the people. They all ate as much as they wanted, and afterward, the disciples picked up twelve baskets of leftovers! Mark 6:30-44. NLT

Jesus did not make the food appear out of thin air, though he could have. In this account he has something to start with. As you work on pushing back fear, realize time and God are on your side, but you must take action.

5. An optimistic worldview. I'm not talking about pie-in-the-sky, but a worldview that has a future-focused path. It means I am not condemned by my past failures; I am not relegated to what I am going to do with my life, based on some test, skill set, or family heritage. It means I have a future I can choose, and with God's grace and work I can have a different life.

Over the past several years the Lord has allowed me the joy of traveling all over the world. I have been in Asia, Europe, the Middle East, Africa, and Baton Rouge, and one of the overwhelming truths I have learned is that we in America experience blessings beyond measure, and we can pursue our dreams. I can tell you from first-hand experience there is not a place in the world like this great country. You have the power, ability, and the opportunity to improve your life if you are willing to take the risk.

The "I'm smarter than the average bear" attitude. I remember hearing a couple of poignant definitions of average. Average is the best of the worst and the worst of the best. Another definition was that average is the cream of the crap.

I have never wanted to settle for average. I'm not the brightest bulb in the box, but I make up for it by being creative and finding ways to be unique and different.

As you look at pushing back fear, I want you to realize you are intentionally designed to leave your mark in the world. Here is my question for you: Are you going to let fear keep you from having a larger impact for God in your life and the life of others? Or, like many people who choose to be "average," will you live a life of regret? I don't want to sound egotistical, but I hope there are a ton of people at my funeral, not to praise me, but to demonstrate the power and influence of a life that wanted to influence people for the Kingdom of God.

My friend, Dr. Charles Lowery, is a gifted speaker, psychologist, and human behavior expert. Several years ago I had the joy of working with him on a church staff in Albuquerque. As a mental health professional and associate pastor, Charles and I had some shared interests from helping people to know Christ and make Him known, to understanding human behavior.

I have heard him speak on the subject of fear many times, and I've always remembered two powerful acrostics that he uses to describe fear:

Forget Everything and Run

False Evidence Appearing Real.

I would like to add a third:

Forever Exploring Another Route.

Think about that for just a minute. Fear almost always causes us to study another path, one that is potentially less damaging and dangerous, but also less rewarding. If you are going to push back fear, you will most likely have to face this tendency to explore another route.

Four Proven Ways to Push Through Fear and Self-Doubt

Self-observation can be a great use of your time if it leads to positive things and not into self-flagellation. I've spent a significant portion of my working life guiding people through self-observation. In that time, I have discovered far too many people on the edge of a breakthrough in their personal life, their relationships, or their business but who squander the opportunity by over-focusing on self-doubt and fear. The thing that surprises me to this day is that many times they are completely unaware of how their self-talk defeats them. Here is how it usually happens. People say they want something very badly, that they want to change, and theoretically, they would do almost anything to make the change and get what they want.

But when it comes time to turn the key, to take the step, it is an entirely different story. For many, when it is time to take action, they get cold feet and either pause or back out and fail to do what they need to do to get the results they want. Why? The usual suspect is the inner self-doubting voice that has them questioning every move they make in experiencing the changes they want to engage.

Would you like to learn practical, concrete ways to push back fear? Here are four methods you can implement to press fear back.

1. *Feel the fear and do it anyway.*

My wife Angie is no fan of heights. She would do almost anything not illegal to avoid heights. However, my wife is a strong woman who does not like to admit defeat. She is involved with an excellent direct service company called Premier Designs Jewelry, and in the year of her sixtieth birthday, she had qualified for a free Caribbean cruise.

One evening, as we were preparing for the journey and looking at different adventures and excursions, she said, "I want to go tandem parasailing at Grand Cayman." I was surprised and yet readily agreed. She went on to say, "I know I need to take action to push back the fear, so let's do this. I am also going to tell some of my close girlfriends what my plan is. That way, I will have positive peer pressure that will hopefully keep me from chickening out."

The day came, and with tons of encouragement, we hopped on the boat and headed out. After watching some other couples take the ride, it was our turn. The air was warm; the breeze was gentle as we slipped into the harness. Within a few seconds, we were gently lifted off the deck, and the winch began to unwind. After a minute or two, we were soaring 400 feet above the water. As we floated, talked, and took it all in, it was inspiring to see the radiance in Angie's face as we looked down on our cruise ship from our airy, highly-harnessed perch in our parasail.

When we landed on the deck of the boat, a couple of our friends gave Angie hugs and high-fives. When all of us returned to the ship that evening, Angie's accountability partners and friends were overjoyed at what she had done and listened intently to her story.

When you feel the fear, call it what it is, and face it, friends will come alongside to pray with you, encourage you, and walk with you.

All of us experience fear from time to time. What separates people who discover success in their lives and those who give permission for fear to hold them back is the willingness to act in spite of the fear.

2. *Make no apologies—no excuses.*

As a young cadet at Georgia Military College in the late 60's, I came under the influence of a seasoned warrior, Command Sergeant Major Scott, one of our military instructors. He was quite a character, soft-spoken but a veteran of WWII, the Korean Conflict, the Dominican Republic Action, and two tours in Viet Nam. When he spoke, everybody listened because of the respect we had for this leader. He was full of pithy quotes, and one I remember to this day is: "Men, if you are looking for an excuse, any one will do. Just remember you are accountable for the decisions you make." I have to admit, as a young man, it didn't make much sense at the time, but over the years, I have come to appreciate the wisdom he shared.

While some call them "reasons," people stop themselves all the time using rationalizations and excuses. The top reasons, particularly in the direct sales business, go something like this: "I don't have time;" I don't know anybody;" My friends and I are too busy." This list goes on.

As Command Sergeant Major Scott said, "When looking for an excuse, any one will do."

People will use excuses like a trap door or an ejection seat—an escape usually based in self-doubt.

One of the ways to have more of what you want and what God wants in your life is to push back fear and self-doubt. To do this, you will need to hone the skill of developing a "no excuses" approach.

So, how bad do you want to change? You can either have "reasons" or life changing results. The choice is always yours.

3. *Be willing to move outside of your comfort zone.*

I have to admit, I honestly admire the wild success of Taylor Swift, but I would never want to be a former boyfriend. In an interview a couple of years ago she was asked about another famous singer who consistently pushed her comfort zone.

Swift said, "One element of Madonna's career that really takes center stage is how many times she's reinvented herself. It is easier to stay in one look, one comfort zone, one musical style. It is exciting to me to see someone whose only predictable quality is being unpredictable."[12]

Here are some other quotes that will help you think about this:

Taylor Swift:

"You have people come into your life shockingly and surprisingly. You have losses you never thought you'd experience. You have rejection, and you have to learn how to deal with that and how to get up the next day and go on with it."

"I think fearless is having fears but jumping anyway."

Joel Olsteen:

"I want to challenge you today to get out of your comfort zone. You have so much incredible potential on the inside. God has put gifts and talents in you (that) you probably don't know anything about."[13]

Bruce Wilkerson:

"It's when you begin to think about going to your dream that your dream is always outside your comfort zone. It is always just beyond what you have ever done."[14]

Adventurer Bear Grylls:

> "Adventure should be 80 percent 'I think it is
> manageable,' but it's good to have 20 percent where
> you are just outside of your comfort zone. Still safe,
> but outside your comfort zone." [15]

Let's face it, most of us avoid discomfort with a passion. If you want to progress in your personal life, your relationships, and your business, you will have to become more familiar with being out of your comfort zone—for a short time. Will it be scary? Yes, but it will not kill you, and it may even make you a better person.

The key question is—are you willing to exchange short-term discomfort for a better life, richer relationships, and a more successful enterprise? If the answer is yes, are you willing to push back the self-doubt and move beyond your comfort zone?

Yes? Here is some great news: blessing, joy and opportunities will increase. So get ready!

4. Just do it!

The biggest difference between daydreaming and having a big dream is action!

Wishful thinking will never get you there. You must engage, take a risk, lean into the self-doubt and fear. You have to "rise from the doubts and fears and walk." This is the place where the phrase "If it is to be, it is up to me," kicks in. This is the "grown up" location where you declare to yourself that you are solely responsible for your life, and you accept the fact you cannot blame others for the choices you have made. Time and time again, this is the place where our negative self-talk, which fuels self-doubt and fear, causes us to question everything and keeps us from taking action. I call it *decision constipation*. This fear and self-doubt are at the bottom of self-sabotage.

Getting a higher and wider vantage point around moving forward with your life starts with a decision. Once you have made that decision, it is time to get down to work and make it happen.

My pastor, Todd Cook, of Sagebrush Community Church in Albuquerque recently introduced a song by Hillary Scott of Lady Antebellum.

Scott recently had to carry a tough burden of her own, having experienced a miscarriage. As a result of working through the pain of the loss, she made peace with it in the months ahead and penned the poignant tune, "Thy Will." The song appears on a gospel album she recorded with her family called *Love Remains*, which was released in July 2016.

This was not Hillary Scott's first challenge.

Did you know that before she joined Lady Antebellum, she auditioned twice for American Idol but failed to make it to the judges' round? After those two failed attempts she, along with Charles Kelley and Dave Haywood, founded Lady Antebellum and the rest is chart-making history.

Nicolette's Story: Have a God-Sized Dream

One of the many aspects of my job is that I am an International Crisis Management Consultant and Crisis Response Specialist. Recently I was on a deployment to the Democratic Republic of Congo. I was "in country." The ominous, heavily armored, black door bore the marks of generations of paint. The bulletproof glass was covered with a colorful African print that reminded me of a dashiki my wife made me back in the 70's.

James and I had visited several times during my TDY, and today he was going to take me to a small Lebanese restaurant. I always enjoyed time with a kindred spirit. James is a career diplomat who is filled like an overflowing cup with joy and excitement about life and his various assignments. James saw every job as an opportunity to learn about the people and the local culture.

As we enjoyed our hummus, tahini, tabbouleh, shawarma, cucumbers and yogurt, and pita bread, he began to tell me about his administrator, Nicolette.

As he told the story of her journey, my draw dropped in both bewilderment and amazement.

The second Congo War, otherwise known as the Great African War, began in 1998 and ended with a peace treaty in 2003. Between 1996 and 2006, 5.4 million people had died. (If you would like to dig a little deeper, read *Dancing in the Glory of the Monsters: The Collapse of the Congo and the Great War of Africa* by Jason K. Stearns).

This is the palette for the story Nicolette shared with me that morning.

During these dangerous days, there was indiscriminate killing, destruction, rape, mutilation, and every other type of corrupt behavior people can do to each other. Men and women were hacked to death. Women and girls were raped, beaten, and forced into sexual slavery. Children were kidnapped, and many were trained as soldiers.

Nicolette lived in the southeastern area of the Eastern Democratic Republic of Congo, and up to this point had managed to survive most of the carnage that was going on around her. As the violence once again began to flare in her region, Nicolette faced a crucial choice— stay and take her chances and live in fear, or leave and hope for a better, safer place to raise her children and make a life for herself. She had an almost impossible God-sized dream.

After much prayer and planning, she made a courageous choice to begin an 800 kilometer (500 mile) trek to freedom and safety.

Nicolette, like so many others in her country, was about to become a refugee. Over the next several months, she and her children began their long walk to safety. Some days they traveled with other refugees. Other times, when they heard that military or rebel patrols were in the area, Nicolette and the children would go into the bush. On some occasions, villagers or relief agencies would provide food; other days she had to count on foraging skills she learned as a little girl living near the jungle.

As she moved into the portion of her story about coming into Goma, she began to tear up and shared how humble and grateful she felt about arriving in this safe town. After walking 800 kilometers, she and the children reconnected with family members who had made room for them and welcomed them with great joy and relief. Her initial dream was accomplished. Like Moses and the children of Israel, she survived her exodus with the combination of hard work, the grace of God, and the kindness of strangers. She and her children finally enjoyed sleeping in real beds, eating regular food, enjoying the company of family and friends.

She felt blessed she had taken the risk, pushed through the fear, and made it to Goma.

She soon began looking for work. Within a few days, she interviewed and was hired as a medical assistant in a facility that treated girls and women who'd been raped, mutilated, and disfigured in many cases by soldiers on both sides of the conflict. Nicolette was not trained as a medical professional, but the nurses and doctors at the facility noted that she had the gift of mercy and was a great listener and encourager. She told me she had listened to hundreds of hours of stories, and had prayed with and encouraged hundreds of girls and women during the time she worked at the facility.

Nicolette shared how important this part of her life was to her. She believed God had led her and spared her to be able to protect her children and to help others. She found a great sense of completeness while providing much-needed encouragement and support to others in this season of her life.

But there was a cost.

As God led her through the circumstances of her life, she moved to Kinshasa, Democratic Republic of Congo and found stable, well-paying work.

More than 200 people had been killed in the eastern part of DRC, In Kinshasa, and there was palpable political pressure as the current president did not want to step down, while most of the population wanted him to go away. With the current political strife and threatened increase in violence, Nicolette made a choice to come and see me.

The massive, armored door to my office was slightly cracked when I heard the muffled thump on the door. It was Nicolette.

She was a humble, gentle woman of faith who was dressed in the bright, bold, traditional colors called *pagne*. Despite the wars, oppression, corrupt government, and challenging history of the Democratic Republic of Congo, along with many other sub-Saharan countries, these dynamic, colorful designs show the strength, resilience, and optimism of the people of the DRC. On this day she also wore a matching headscarf. Her outfit helped me see some of the inner strength this woman possessed.

As we exchanged *bonjours*, she mentioned she liked my accent as I made an attempt to give an appropriate greeting.

We sat down, and I asked how I could help her. She replied, "I have been having great difficulty sleeping and concentrating at work and home." I absorbed her words, intonation, and nonverbal cues to discern what she was trying to tell me. After a short pause, I asked her to share her story with me. For the next several minutes she brought to light some of the parts of her journey, her work in Goma, how her faith had grown, and how much better her life was today.

Her mood and eyes suddenly became sad and tearful. She began to tell me about the flashbacks and memories she was currently having. She thought she'd put these behind her. As she continued to share her burden, I gently asked a few more questions. She told me that with all of the rising political dissent and the troubles in the eastern part of the country, she was afraid war would break out again.

It was evident she was dealing with some PTSD issues. But with the status of mental health in this part of the world, we needed to look for some practical things she could do until there could be an appropriate referral.

I asked her to tell me more about her faith and how it had helped her. I shared a few things about PTSD and how to manage it. One of the truths I shared was the importance of finding meaning in the traumatic event. I also mentioned a phrase that intrigued her: "Don't waste the pain."

As Nicolette opened up, she began to articulate how she believed it was part of God's plan to take the long walk, to work in the hospital with all of those girls and women, and to hold the job she has today. During the questioning, I hoped she would be able to see how the Lord was leading and guiding her through all the ups and downs she had experienced.

It was an almost miraculous moment when I watched the light bulb turn on. Nicolette sat up straight, with a hope-filled, determined look as a smile slowly revealed itself. She said, "I get it. God was there all along, He is with me now, and will be with me in the future." She went on to tell me how much better she felt. With that, our session ended. Over the next several days she checked in a couple of times to tell me how much better she was doing.

What motivated her to take the risks that she did for herself and her children? What big dream did she have to help her find the faith, courage, resilience, and grace to make this trip happen?

First, like many ordinary people who accomplish incredible things with their lives, she had the almost impossible dream of getting her family to a safer place.

Second, she developed a plan with options to make it happen. She worked her plan, and was prepared for the possible adversity that lay ahead. Looking back, she noted, "I learned many lessons as a child that would teach me how to provide for my family on the darkest of days."

Third, she trusted God and served others. And while there is some residual pain as a result of this arduous journey, she is a stronger, more faithful servant of God for taking the trip.

She continues to enjoy working with James and the rest of her team. She is also actively involved in her church and ministers to girls and women in her community.

I will never forget the enduring strength of this incredible lady. When I have fears or troubles, I will remember her godly example.

Nicolette's motivation, her God-sized dream gave her the courage to push through her fear and provide for her family.

That same spirit lives in you!

Here are some proven things you can do to make it happen:

Know your "why." Nicolette's "why" was to give her children a chance to grow up in a safer place in order to have a better life.

Expand your "dream." Her dream was to get to a safe place.

Write it down. Everyone has dreams for their future. It might be to write a book, start a new hobby or venture, or to make some life changes. A great way to bring a more concrete feeling to these dreams is by making a dream board, also known as a vision board. A dream board (or vision board) is a visual tool that serves as a guide to your goals for the future. It is a visual representation of your dreams and your ideal life. - [3] Making your own unique dream board can be a chance to explore your own goals and dreams and exercise your creativity.

Share the idea with people you trust. The accountability will be an excellent source of help and encouragement. Nicolette did share her plans with a few friends, who agreed to pray with her.

Get a coach, mentor, or accountability partner to help you develop a plan.

DO IT! Nicolette did it.

Stressed brains don't work too well.

In the 1960's, a young psychologist, named Dr. Marty Seligman and his colleagues were doing research on classical conditioning or the process of how animals and humans associate one thing with something else. While this type of investigation is no longer allowed, Seligman and his team were able to more deeply understand "learned helplessness." Learned helplessness is when people feel helpless to avoid adverse situations because of previous experience has shown them they do not have control.

Here is the beautiful German Shepherd, lying in the corner of a metal box, whimpering. He receives painful shocks that leave him writhing in pain. Oddly enough, the dog could easily escape. The opposite side of the box is completely insulated from shocks, and there is only a small barrier, which the dog could hop or step over to escape the pain. Though the dog could jump over to safety whenever he wishes, he doesn't. He lies down and takes the hit, crying out with each unexpected jolt. He must be physically moved by the experimenter to be relieved of the experience.[16]

How could this happen?

A few days before the experiment, the dog was strapped to a restraining harness rigged with electrical wires, inescapably receiving the same painful shock day and night. At first, he didn't just stand still and take it, he reacted. He howled with pain. He urinated. He strained mightily against his harness with heroic, but desperate attempts. But all attempts were useless. As the hours and the days went by, his resistance eventually surrendered. How did this happen? The dog began to receive a message that was clear: the pain wasn't going to stop. The shocks were going to last forever. *There was no way out.* Even after the dog has been released from the harness and placed into the metal box with an escape route, he could no longer understand he had options. Learning had been entirely shut down.

What is so awful about severe, chronic stress or fear is that it can cause behavioral, physical, and spiritual changes as devastating as learned helplessness.

Can you and I agree that fear can be a great source of stress? If that is the case, then what does fear look like?

Stress is a concept borrowed from engineering. It can be defined as the amount of resistance a material offers to be reshaped or reformed. Walter B. Cannon and Hans Selye were researchers in stress physiology. Cannon developed the fight or flight phenomenon to describe the stress response, and Selye used the term stress to describe the general unpleasantness his lab rats were experiencing when he would routinely drop, chase, and recapture them during his experiments. Selye noticed the rats had a similar set of responses to a broad array of stressors and extended exposure to general unpleasantness made them sick.

Jeansok Kim and David Diamond developed a three-part definition of stress in humans:

A physiological response to the stressor, measurable by another party.

A desire to avoid the situation: the fear must be seen as aversive—something one would rather not experience.

A loss of control: The person does not feel like they have control of the stressor. As the volume knob of an emotional radio, the more loss of control, the more severe the fear of the stress will be .[17]

Chronic fear and stress will hamper life and limit the brain's ability to problem-solve and grow.

So the questions are: Do I allow my fears to lead me down the path to learned helplessness, or are there some things I can learn to do to push back the fear?

Do I want to remain caged by my fear or move into a life that is charged with a dream and a sense of adventure?

Am I comfortable with how I am managing my fears and the stress that comes with that or do I want to charge forward with my faith and a dream and experience the more God might have for me?

Do you, like the dog in this experiment, feel caged, trapped, stuck? Not sure?

People who have become caged tend to be withdrawn and frustrated. Their language is usually laced with phrases like, "They don't understand me," "No one really knows me." Eventually, because of their resistance to change and ever-increasing, brooding anger, people begin to pull back from them and the caged become even more isolated.

If you look underneath what they are saying, it sounds more like they are narcissistic. People believe their pain, fear, or whatever it is that is holding them back makes them unique. This belief is totally against reality.

When a person is looking for an excuse, any one will do. They tend to build their own cages.

So what does this have to do with pushing back my fear? I am glad you asked. Truthfully, only two types of actions will motivate you to push back fear. The first is external motivation, something outside of you motivates you to change the path you are on. The second is internal motivation. Something deep inside comes alive, and you have a new-found hunger, a re-awakened dream, a desire to leave this world a better place than when you came.

While my goal is to give you practical information on understanding the different types of fear we identified in the survey, as well as "best practices" for pushing back fear, the most important thing I can do is provide you with some homework designed to get you into God's Word and point you to the truth that will help you on an even deeper level.

In each chapter, I will give two or three verses to help you take steps to "hide God's Word in your heart."

Bible Study Helps

For God did not give us a spirit of timidity (of cowardice, of craven and clinging), but [He has given us a spirit] of power and of love and well-balanced mind and discipline and self-control 2 Timothy 1:7 (NLT)

According to this passage, what does *not* come from God?

_____

_____

_____

_____

Which one do you most identify with? And why did you choose this one?

_____

_____

_____

_____

What has God has given us, according to this verse?

_____

_____

_____

_____

Based on this passage, as well as some of the sections of this chapter, what steps can you begin doing today to push back the fear? Take a few moments to review this chapter and jot down what you are going to do.

_____

_____

_____

_____

_____

_____

_____

_____

Chapter 2
The Fear of Criticism

The fear of criticism robs a person of their initiative, destroys imaginations, limits initiative, destroys dreams, steals self-reliance, and does, Lord only knows how much more damage. [18]
~Napoleon Hill

During his presidency, Abraham Lincoln was greatly respected and greatly reviled. Blamed for plunging this nation into a civil war, he was the president people loved to hate. Those who opposed his views regarding the war and slavery, as well as his efforts to keep them united, were vocal and uninhibited in denouncing him.

One day during one of the darkest periods of his presidency, Lincoln was walking down a street near the Capitol in Washington when an acquaintance caught up with him. As they walked, the man brought up the subject of the growing anti-Lincoln sentiment flowing in Washington and throughout the country.

With brutal honesty, the man related to Lincoln many of the stories outlining attacks on Lincoln and his policies. As the man spoke, Lincoln remained completely silent and absorbed in his own thoughts.

Then Lincoln stopped, looked directly at the man and said: "Yes, I have heard you, but let me tell you a story. You know that it is the habit of all dogs to come at the night and bark and bark and bark at the moon. This keeps on as long as the moon is clearly visible in the sky."

Then he stopped speaking and continued his walk. Confused by Lincoln's response, his exasperated companion persisted. "Mr. Lincoln, you haven't finished your story. Tell me that rest of it!"

Once again Lincoln stopped walking and said, "There is nothing more to say. The moon keeps right on shining."[19]

President Lincoln is an excellent role model for managing criticism. Although he was aware of his shortcomings and knew many highly respected and influential people disagreed with him, the president listened to the criticism and followed his own intuitive sense that his policies would eventually win over critics and unify the country.

One of life's challenging realities is that there are always people around who are our fault-finders, people who seldom see the good but are quick to point out the negative. Like Abraham Lincoln, all of us need to find ways of hearing criticism without being detracted or destroyed by it.

Fear of Criticism

Fear of criticism is an enormous challenge for many entrepreneurs.

Dr. Seuss said, "Be who you are and say what you feel, because those who mind don't matter and those who matter don't mind."[20]

I love this quote from Darrell Stetler II, a Methodist Pastor in Kentucky: "One of the most natural things humans do is be afraid of what other people will think. You may not believe this affects you... you might not be a part of something like this: Are you a member of the 'Dependent Order of Really Meek and Timid Souls'? The acrostic of the first letters of its name form the word "doormats." The Doormats have an official insignia—a yellow caution light. The official motto is: 'The meek shall inherit the earth if that's ok with everybody!'"

Have you ever caught yourself in the mind trap of "If I am 'perfect' with my actions, no one will criticize me"? Have you ever noticed how tough this is to pull off? If you try and live like a chameleon around everybody, hoping to keep them all happy, you will end up tired, frustrated, and hurt. I bet even as you are reading these words you are feeling your heartbeat increase.

When people are excessively afraid of criticism, they tend to overcompensate in their actions at the expense of what is critical about life connection, compassion, love, and open-heartedness.

Some of the devastating, adverse, and crippling effects related to the fear of criticism include:

Abandoning your dream.

Playing it safe by holding your cards close and minimizing any risk.

Being overly defensive when real friends offer helpful advice or constructive criticism.

Becoming shy and introverted out of fear that others might not want to hear your opinion. So you keep your opinion to yourself.

The general theme of someone who is fearful of criticism is that they are afraid of being real. These fears can lead to an individual to become critical of others, and as a result, the fear that others are judging and criticizing. Therefore, one can fear expressing themselves.

Josie's Story

Josie had been involved with an excellent direct sales/service company for the past eight months. She was an outstanding company rep. Her hostesses loved her; she was always dressed to the hilt and her displays rivaled those at Macy's. Each month she was in the top 25 producers in sales. Her accomplishments had been recognized publicly at both local and regional team meetings and she was one of the companies rising stars. Her husband, Jake, was very supportive of her and gladly took care of their two sons when she was doing her home shows. She loved the money; she'd recently given a nice donation to her church's youth group for a mission trip to Juarez, Mexico. But something seemed off.

She called her up-line leader, who had been in business for several years, and asked for coaching in sponsoring. (Like many home-based businesses, there are at least two ways to generate income. The first is to sell a product, good, or service. The second is to sponsor or recruit and train others to do what you are doing.)

Josie and Becky met the next day at their neighborhood Starbucks for their coaching session. Becky asked a few questions about Josie's husband and the children and then asked, "How can I help you today?" Josie was ready to talk.

She told Becky how much she loved the business and was enjoying the increased cash flow and recognition. However, she was having a difficult time sponsoring. Becky listened patiently, as she had many times before with other ladies in the business. After fifteen minutes of giving her full attention, she asked Josie, "Do you feel like you have to be the perfect representative?"

Josie was completely caught off guard with this question. She had not seen where Becky was headed until that powerfully pointed question pierced her heart. Her eyes teared up.

Becky leaned in and gently touched Josie's arm, comforting her very much like a favorite aunt or big sister.

For the next several minutes, Josie opened up and shared about her upbringing in a home with an absent dad and an overbearing mom. Sure, dad had provided an excellent lifestyle, a lovely home, the best schools, wonderful vacations, but she never felt like she quite measured up. Her mom, on the other hand, was her constant critic, because she wasn't like her older sister who was prettier and smarter. Because of this, Josie had decided to spend her high school years participating in school productions and show choir. In that process, Josie had learned to appear to have her act together, not allowing anyone in so no one would know how scared she was of criticism.

As Josie shared her heart wounds, Becky listened intently. For years Becky had wanted to be involved in Women's Ministry, and she smiled to herself as she reflected on how the Lord was using her business as a Women's Ministry. Because of her business, she could spend her time encouraging, supporting, and loving women like Josie.

As they finished their time together, Becky prayed with Josie and gave her an assignment. They would reconnect the following week.

Josie's assignment was to talk with two or three of her hostesses and ask them why they were reluctant to sign up as a representative when they had indicated an interest at their home show.

Josie called Kat and Shanti, with whom she had been friends for several years. She was somewhat surprised by their answers. They both loved Josie and gave her their feedback. "We love the products, but you come across as almost being perfect. Perfectly dressed, clearly articulate, and almost over-organized, and both of us feel like we can never be that. If your company wants us to look, act, and dress like we completely have our stuff together, then we are not interested."

Needless to say, that rocked Josie's world.

She sent Becky a quick text, "I feel like the wind got knocked out of me!" Becky some encouraged Josie and set a meeting for Monday. Becky knew she didn't need to stay on the phone to "talk Josie down." Instead, she had the wisdom to give Josie time to consider the input she had received.

Monday couldn't come quickly enough for Josie. When they met, Becky asked Josie to share any insights she had gained from talking with Kat and Shanti. Josie, fighting back tears, said, "I am so scared of criticism that I guess I come across as someone who has it all together. But I know I don't have it all together." Even as she shared this with Becky, she could feel the tightness in her chest relax as she let out her secret.

As she and Becky wrapped up the meeting, Becky suggested she lighten up a little.

Over the next few weeks, Josie began to make adjustments, was more open with her hostesses about her struggles, which allowed them to see her as just another flawed person trying to build a home-based business so she could be a stay at home mom. Within a few weeks, she began to sponsor other women into her business. Within the next several months both Kat and Shanti had decided to join Josie.

At the next regional rally, Becky and Josie were on their way to freshen up when Josie told Becky that for the first time in her life, she felt like she could just be herself.

When Josie showed her vulnerability as appropriate at her home shows, she found that women admired her, respected her, and were more likely to want to build a business with her.

Working hard to make sure no one criticizes you is silly and emotionally draining. It is an energy thief stealing from more critical areas in both your personal and business life. There is no right way, just each individual's way.

You cannot escape criticism. With that in mind, let's get to basics. You and I are unique, one-of-a-kind creatures with an excellent combination of talents, skills, and personality. Not everyone will like us or what we say. It's more damaging to worry about being criticized than to handle the criticism.

You were born an original. Don't die a copy. People will criticize you. Bottom line, you must choose to be the unique, authentic self God created you to be and risk the criticism.

When someone criticizes you, you have an option: you can take it to heart or let it "roll off your back." That's your choice. Receiving criticism takes a lot of work and grace. When you learn how to hear criticism, evaluate it, and then decide whether to internalize it or throw it in the trash, you are strengthening your commitment to living the life God intends you to have. When you do this, you put yourself in the driver's seat, taking your power back, and you begin to live in reality and move out of denial. It is a choice that will help you break free of the chain that has held you back.

Before we jump into tips for pushing back fear, I want to share something personal with you. Many people see me as an outgoing, fun-loving, truth-telling, confident Christ follower. And while I am, I have struggled for years with the fear of criticism. Earlier in my life, many times I would find myself trying to figure out which way the wind was blowing around certain groups and try to fit in. And guess what? It never worked.

Once I began to accept the fact that this fear was a big deal in my life, I began to make changes. I also began to study what had worked for other people.

These tips do not come from "book learning," although, with a Bachelor's and two Master's degrees, I have done a lot of "book learning." These practical, proven tips, which I believe are rooted in the truth of the Scriptures, will help you push back this fear if you put them to work.

Six Tips for Dealing with Criticism

Tip #1—People are going to criticize you no matter what you do. So why not give them something to talk about? As you grow, become more visible, and share your gifts, vision, and expertise, others will criticize.

As you step into this adventure of pushing back the fear of criticism you will only have two options:

Option #1— Gripe, complain, moan and groan. Complain about how unfair things are and how we should all just love and respect each other. FYI: This will do nothing but make you more miserable.

Option #2— Accept the fact that people will be critical which doesn't mean you have to like it or let people walk all over you. Once you have done that, then take what you need and dismiss the rest.

Tip #2—Learn to look inside and discover the beautiful person God created you to be.

Recently, I attended the Fellowship Church in Gonzales, Louisiana and heard an excellent sermon about the Woman at the Well in John 4:4-42. Read it today; I promise you will be blessed.

This story is only in John's gospel, and it is about a nameless Samaritan woman's encounter with Jesus, the longest one-on-one conversation of Jesus recorded in Bible. This interaction gives us brilliant insight into how the Lord sees us, warts and all.

She was a Samaritan, a group of folks who were hated by the Jews of Jesus's time. In addition, she was an outcast from her own culture, marked as an immoral woman, five times divorced, living with a man who wasn't her husband.

I just love how Jesus read her mail and identified her and her actions, yet did not condemn, belittle, gossip about, or disrespect her. Instead, this immoral woman, who would probably be labeled a sex addict today, was one of the early people to whom he disclosed his true identity.

As a result, Jesus's encounter with the Woman at the Well teaches us that God loves us in spite of our corrupt lives. God values us enough to actively seek us, to welcome us to intimacy, and to rejoice in worship. And God uses our brokenness to bring others into relationship with Himself. As a result of this conversation and the woman's testimony, scores of Samaritans came into a relationship with Christ.

People believe two lies. The first is that our sense of self-esteem should be based on our performance. The second is that our self-esteem is based on what others think about us.

Now, while it is important to be the best employee you can be in the workplace, that has nothing to do with healthy self-esteem.

A healthy sense of self-worth is based on God's love for me; he knows how bad I can mess things up and yet He chooses to love me and be a dynamic part of my life if I allow Him to be. He gives me a purpose for living.

Tip #3—Listen to your inner critic and disagree. Learn to challenge your thoughts. In 2 Corinthians 10:3-5 (NLT) we read:

> *We are human, but we don't wage war as humans do.*
> *We use God's mighty weapons, not worldly weapons, to*

knock down the strongholds of human reasoning and to destroy false arguments. We destroy every proud obstacle that keeps people from knowing God. We capture their rebellious thoughts and teach them to obey Christ.

Paul uses a military term to describe this warfare with sin and Satan. God must be the leader, even of our thought lives. The idea of walking circumspectly is being situationally aware of your thoughts, your "at risk" areas of life, where you can be tempted. When these thoughts—even self-defeating thoughts—come to mind, capture it and give it to Jesus. When we are exposed to toxic thinking or toxic behaviors, we always have a choice. My challenge to you is to recognize the danger, the self-defeating thoughts and actions, and refuse to let them take hold of you. Instead, ask God to give you discernment and find a trusted friend who can encourage you.

Tip #4—Remember, you're an adult, and you get to choose. Choose wisely.

Tip #5—Don't be intimidated by criticism. Look for wisdom in criticism. When people who love you are critical, trust that they love you and have your best interest in mind. Cut them some slack and meet them with an open heart and mind.

Tip #6—Move from being emotionally fragile to emotional resilient.

Bible Study Helps
Be guided by wisdom of other leaders

Love your enemies! Pray for those who persecute you!
Matthew 5:44 (NLT)

I am sure you have heard a part of the Serenity Prayer, but very few have looked at the full prayer.

Your assignment for this section: Read this prayer.

The Complete Serenity Prayer
by Reinhold Niebuhr

God, grant me the Serenity to accept the things I cannot change, the Courage to change the things I can, and the Wisdom to know the difference.

Living one day at a time; Enjoying one moment at a time; Accepting hardship as the pathway to peace.

Taking, as He did, this sinful world as it is, not as I would have it.

Trusting He will make all things right if I surrender to His Will;

That I may be reasonably happy in this life, and supremely happy with Him forever in the next.

Amen.

Now take a few minutes to reflect on this verse from Isaiah 41:10

Don't be afraid, for I am with you.
Don't be discouraged, for I am your God.
I will strengthen you and help you.
I will hold you up with my victorious right hand. (NLT)

What does the Lord tell us to stop doing?

_____

_____

_____

_____

What does He want to do for you?

_____

_____

_____

_____

List what you can do to begin to implement the truths you read today?

_____

_____

_____

_____

Chapter 3
The Fear of Failure

Failure should be our teacher, not our undertaker.
Failure is a delay, not defeat. It is a temporary detour,
not a dead-end. Failure is something we can avoid only
by saying nothing, doing nothing, and being nothing.[21]
~Denis Waitley

Failures are finger posts on the road to achievement. [22]
~C.S. Lewis

When you act out of fear, your fears come true. Fears about creativity fall into two families—worries about yourself, and fears about your reception by others. In a general way, fears about yourself prevent you from doing your best work, while fear of your reception by others prevents you from doing your work at all.

I have experienced this as a photographer. I've taken photos for years, and have even been paid for some of it. For me, photography is my creative outlet. It gives me an opportunity to express myself and do things that are personally rewarding. It is also a venue for displaying God's creation in both humanity and nature.

For years, family and friends asked me where I showed my art, or if I ever entered art contests. I would usually make a lame excuse, which worked pretty well until a photographer friend of mine who is a pro and mentor got in my head. She suggested reading *Art &Fear: Observations on the Perils (and Rewards) of Artmaking*. I did, and I highly recommend it to anyone who is creative and yet fearful about sharing their art. It helped me realize that my art is my art and there are people who want to see what I do with my creative process. (I remember Jesus saying something about not putting a light under a bushel in Matthew 5:15.)

I believe one of the most powerful ways we can push back the fear of failure is to read about and observe how others have overcome this game-stopping fear, glean the lessons they learned, and apply them to our life as appropriate.

Did you know?

> • **Michael Jordan** missed more than half of the shots he took. "I've missed more than 9,000 shots in my career. I've lost almost 300 games. Twenty-six times I've been trusted to take the game-winning shot and missed. I've failed over and over and over again in my life. And that is why I succeed."[23]

> • **J.K. Rowling**. The *Harry Potter* author's story is legendary. She wrote *Harry Potter and the Philosopher's Stone* (the first book of the series) as a struggling single welfare mom and had twelve rejections from publishers. Her first book eventually sold for the equivalent of $4,000.00. She says, "Failure is so important. We speak about success all the time. It is the ability to resist failure or use failure which often leads to greater success. I've met people who don't want to try for fear of failing... Failure meant a stripping away of the inessential. I stopped pretending to myself that I was anything other than what I was and began diverting all my energy into finishing the only work that mattered to me."[24]

Today, based on her book sales and incredible film series she is now worth over $1 billion dollars.

> • **Winston Churchill** failed the sixth grade and lost every public election he entered until being elected Prime Minister of Great Britain at age 62. "Success is stumbling from failure to failure with no loss of

enthusiasm…Success is not final; failure is not fatal: it is the courage to continue that counts."[25]

• **Charlize Theron.** When Theron was 15, she witnessed her mother shoot her alcoholic father in an act of self-defense. Instead of letting the trauma immobilize her ambition, Theron channeled her energy into making a name for herself. She would eventually become one of the most respected and talented actresses, becoming the first South African actress to win an Academy Award.[26]

• **Stephenie Meyer.** Before the *Twilight* series broke sales records, she faced the failure of rejection—multiple times. Meyer wrote fifteen letters to various literary agents and received fourteen rejections. Fortunately, one agent took her on and eight publishers bid on the rights to publish her wildly successful series which turned into a highly popular movie franchise.[27]

• **Vera Wang's** path to becoming the successful designer she is today was by no means conventional. First, Wang, who was a competitive skater in her youth, failed to make the 1968 U.S. Olympic Figure Skating Team. To the benefit of the fashion industry, this loss of a dream prompted her to take a job as an assistant at Vogue in 1971, where she was eventually promoted to senior fashion editor within a year—at age 23! After fifteen years with the magazine, Wang was passed over for the editor-in-chief position. But she ended up where she needed to be and has become one of the leading fashion designers of all time.[28]

None of these people would have made history if they had chosen to be frozen by failure.

I do not know anyone who enjoys failing. For some people, the fear of failing can present such an overwhelming psychological menace that their incentive to *avoid failure* exceeds their motivation to succeed. This very personal and intimidating fear of failure causes them to unintentionally sabotage their chances of success in a broad variety of ways.

Failure can stir up feelings of disappointment, anger, sadness, regret, frustration, disappointment, and confusion. Underneath this fear is a deeper fear of shame. People who have a fear of failure are motivated to avoid failing, not because they cannot manage the underlying emotions of disappointment, anger, and frustration that accompany such experiences, but because failing makes them feel a profound sense of shame.

Indicators for Fear of Failure

1. You worry about your ability to go after your dreams.

2. You worry about what others think of you.

3. You feel if people knew you they would reject you.

4. You consistently live in a world of lowered expectation.

5. Once you have experienced failure at something, you have difficulty imagining what you could have done differently.

6. You often get last minute headaches, stomach aches, or other distressing physical symptoms which keep you from finishing the task at hand.

7. Failure makes you doubt your abilities and how smart or capable you are.

So, with all this knowledge, what are practical ways to overcome the fear of failure?

Always remember: regrets are worse than failures. Jack Canfield says it well, "Everything you want is on the other side of fear."

Author L.R. Knost puts it this way:

> "When lying in bed at night and regrets from the day
> come to steal your sleep:
> > 'I should have.'
> > 'If only I'd.'
> > 'I wished I'd;'
> grab one of them and turn it around into an 'I will'
> and sleep peacefully knowing that tomorrow will be a
> better day."[29]

Seek out the cause. Where does your fear of failure originate? Understanding the cause is the first step in coming to terms with our fear.

Most people will not need a therapist to do this. Take a couple of minutes to think about a pair of "failure messages" in your life.

Got it? What are you thinking? What is your feeling?

Here is a little secret that I teach in my seminars. It is called the ATC method. If you can grasp this tip, I can promise you will discover newfound freedom.

Here is a test to show you how it works:

A

You smell warm cookies fresh from the oven. That is the A – the trigger event.

T

Your first thought might be something like, "This reminds me of my mother or grandmother." Hopefully, that is a pleasant memory. This is the T for thoughts.

C

Here are the Consequences. You feel a positive memory, comfort, or some other pleasant sensation.

Your behavioral response is that you eat one.

A is an activating event, a trigger event.

T represents the immediate thought which the activating event provokes. The happy thought--happy outcome, unhappy thought—unhappy result.

C is the consequences—the results of the thought. They are twofold

      1. First, a feeling.

      2. Second, the behavioral response.

(Go to my website: www.johnthurman.net and link to my free video on the ATC's.)

(WARNING: Don't spend too much time on this. Identifying the trigger/s will help you overcome them.)

Stay focused on your "Why."

To overcome the fear of failure, set your focus on the goal, dream, or outcome that you want to create. The more you focus with the end in mind, the less power you will give fear.

Recognize avoidance patterns, self-sabotaging, and push forward. Once you shift your mindset from being a victim to an overcomer who is in pursuit of your dreams, you are moving forward. When fear holds you, you tend to either avoid or waste time on the mundane things of life.

"Never, never, never quit!" This famous line comes from Winston Churchill in the earl days of World War II. Churchill was the Prime Minister of England at the time. In those dark days England was being bombed on a daily basis and civilians were dying throughout the island nation.

It was in this context that the following short speech was made on BBC in October of 1941:

Never give in—never, never, never, never, in nothing great or small, large or petty, never give in except to

convictions of honor and good sense. Never yield to force; never yield to the apparently overwhelming might of the enemy.
~Winston Churchill

One of the keys to winning at anything you do is to be persistent—to never quit.

"Where there is no vision, people perish." Taken from Proverbs 29:18, this passage points to the truth that if we have no vision, no path, no idea where we want to go, we will never arrive. To push back fear you have to be crystal clear about what your goal or dream is.

Trust Your Dream. If you believe that the Lord has given you a dream or desire to do something, just do it. If He gave you the dream, He will provide the tools to fulfill it. The secret? You have to open the tool box and get to work.

Break Your Dreams into Bite-Sized Portions. To succeed at anything from weight loss to increasing your personal productivity, you have to figure out what your goal is and what steps you will have to take to make it happen.

Have a long-term view, realizing that there will be ups and downs. A can-do attitude helps us never give up on the dreams that God has placed in our hearts. Focus allows us to recharge, reinvest, and reinvent ourselves by melting down our fear.

Share Your Dreams and Your Fears. In my work as a Crisis Response Specialist, I tell people that one of the keys to moving through a traumatic event is to remember that "Pain shared is pain divided; Joy shared is joy multiplied" (LTC David Grossman). When we do this with our trusted friends we will find the courage, faith, and support to push through the fear and go after our God-sized dream.

Patience, Faith, and Friends are Our Best Allies.

Choose to shift into a "growth mindset." Dr. Carol Dweck, the author of Mindset[30], spent her life researching the origins of mindsets, their role in motivation and self-regulation, and their impact on achievement and interpersonal processes. Her findings give us two options—a growth mindset or a fixed mindset.

A "fixed mindset" is one in which you believe you are born with a particular set of talents, abilities, and intelligence—all of which are unchangeable. Some people with a fixed mindset may find it harder to experience life change and growth. As a result, a fixed-mindset person fails to develop his abilities and is more likely to give up or become distracted and feel depressed when he fails to make the grade in his own eyes.

A person with a growth mindset begins in a different place. When you have a growth mindset you see yourself and others as more flexible, adaptable, and hopeful. Way down inside, you know the potential for growth and development. With the right motivation, effort, moral compass, and concentration you believe you can become better at almost anything. A person who has a growth mindset doesn't take failure personally. That individual tends to see failure as an opportunity for growth. If one path doesn't work, then the person will try another.

As a Christian therapist, I believe the Bible continually teaches the benefit of being growth-minded. I believe God is active in time, space, and history and that He has an active, life-fulfilling plan for each of us. The Bible gives us truth, hope, and stories of those who have gone before us and have found such purpose.

You can overcome the fear of failure by understanding those old triggers and turning them from energy sapping vampires into life-motivating power that will help you accomplish your dreams.

A Look at the Proverbs 31 Woman and the Parable of the Talents

The Proverbs 31 woman and Jesus' Parable of the Talents give us interesting insights that show bold initiative—not timid passivity—is what real faith is all about.

I have always been amazed at what happens when the discussion topic is business, money, or even success. Many Christians grow uncomfortable about those issues, particularly when someone starts to think and talk about finding a better job or starting a new business. Frequently, someone will pull the "super spiritual" card and attempt to correct the person who is wanting more out of life. I am afraid sometimes people think passivity equals faith.

Scriptures show such a different view of faith and business success.

First, the Proverbs 31 woman. Please read it a couple of times, without commentaries or Bible Study aids. Just see what it says.

- She is virtuous and capable; she is completely trusted by her husband, and she enriches his life.

- She is in the fashion business and a great cook.

- She is successful in the real estate business and is a profitable farmer.

- She is energetic and a hard worker. She makes sure all her dealings are profitable.

- She has no fear of being poor.

- She is not someone who sits around watching Christian television and listening to Christian radio, or running from one Bible Study to another. She is involved in her culture, is respected by the community, and is successful.

- She is not afraid of failure. As a matter of fact, she has a very broad portfolio with multiple income streams.

The fear of failure is nothing new. Take a look at the Parable of the Talents found in Matthew 25:14-30. First, a point of clarity on what a talent is. In this context, it is not a skill; it is not a gift. A talent is a weight measure of money. It is roughly 75 pounds. Now if we use the current price of silver per ounce—$17.61—and multiply $17.61 x 16 oz. ($281.76), then multiply that by 75 lbs., one talent would today be worth $21,132.00.

A second more broadly interpreted view of the talents refers to all the gifts, natural abilities, and resources God has given each of us.

So with that, let's take a few minutes and examine this familiar parable with fresh eyes.

The parables of Jesus teach eternal truth while offering practical lessons for living in the world. This powerful, practical Parable of the Talents is told in Matthew 25:14-30. Going back to my days at seminary, my New Testament professor was quick to point out that with parables, there are multiple layers to the story. While Jesus used illustrations that were familiar to His listeners, these verbal images were used to point to deeper things. Regarding the fear of failure, this parable is a story of capital, investment, entrepreneurship, and the appropriate use of scarce economic resources.

"A wealthy man was headed out for a long journey and called three of his servants together. He told them they would be caretakers of his property while he was away. The master had carefully considered the natural abilities of each servant. He gave one five talents ($105,660.00), two ($42,264.00) to another, and one ($21,132.00) to the third, each according to their ability. The master left on his journey.

"After a long time, their master returned from his trip and called them to give an account of how they had used his money. The servant to whom he had entrusted the five bags of silver came forward with five more and said, 'Master, you gave me five bags of silver to invest, and I have earned five more.'

"The master was full of praise. 'Well done, my good and faithful servant. You have been faithful in handling this small amount, so now I will give you many more responsibilities. Let's celebrate together!'

"The servant who had received the two bags of silver came forward and said, 'Master, you gave me two bags of silver to invest, and I have earned two more.'

"The master said, 'Well done, my good and faithful servant. You have been faithful in handling this small amount, so now I will give you many more responsibilities. Let's celebrate together!'

"Then the servant with the one bag of silver came and said, 'Master, I knew you were a harsh man, harvesting crops you didn't plant and gathering crops you didn't cultivate. I was afraid I would lose your money, so I hid it in the earth. Look, here is your money back.'

"But the master replied, 'You wicked and lazy servant! If you knew I harvested crops I didn't plant and gathered crops I didn't cultivate, why didn't you deposit my money in the bank? At least I could have gotten some interest on it.'

"Then he ordered, 'Take the money from this servant, and give it to the one with the ten bags of silver. To those who use well what they are given, even more will be given, and they will have an abundance. But from those who do nothing, even what little they have will be taken away. Now throw this useless servant into outer darkness, where there will be weeping and gnashing of teeth.'

This parable includes a critical lesson about how we are to use our God-given capacities and resources. In the book of Genesis, God gave Adam and Eve the Earth in which to labor for their use. In the parable, the master expected his servants to seek material gain. Rather than passively preserve what they had been given, they were supposed to invest the money. The master was angry at the timidity of the servant who had received the one talent. God commands us to use our talents toward productive ends. The parable emphasizes the need for work and creativity as opposed to idleness.

Here are five truths for you to consider from this powerful parable:

First, this parable teaches us that accomplishment or success is a product of our work.

Many in the church today see their salvation as a "fire insurance policy that will get them to heaven." They believe it doesn't matter what they do between the time they got "saved' and the time they die. This parable clearly instructs what we are supposed to do while we await the return of the Messiah.

We are to work, using our talents, money, gifts, and business opportunities to glorify God, to serve the common good, and to invest in the expansion of God's Kingdom. A biblical view of success is working diligently in the here and now using everything God has given us to produce the return expected by the Master.

Let me be clear here: There is nothing I can do to save myself. I cannot be good enough. I cannot make a deal with God. The Apostle Paul says it best.

> *God saved you by his grace when you believed. And you can't take credit for this; it is a gift from God. Salvation is not a reward for the good things we have done, so none of us can boast about it. For we are God's masterpiece. He has created us anew in Christ Jesus, so we can do the good things he planned for us long ago.* Ephesians 2:8-10 (NLT)

The Book of James, particularly the second chapter, mentions that, while faith is a gift, fruit is expected.

> *Now someone may argue, "Some people have faith; others have good deeds." But I say, "How can you show me your faith if you don't have good deeds? I will show you my faith by my good deeds."* James 2:18 (NLT)

Second, the Parable of the Talents teaches us that the Lord gives us everything we need to do what He has called us to do.

Just as the master counted upon his servants to do more than passively preserve what had been entrusted to them, so God expects us to generate a return by using the gifts, talents, abilities, and opportunities He has given us. The Apostle Paul says in Ephesians 2:10 (NLT),

> *For we are God's masterpiece. He has created us anew in Christ Jesus, so we can do the good things he planned for us long ago.*

Third, the Parable of the Talents teaches that we are not all created equal. One of the most often overlooked verses in the parable is the second part of verse fifteen: The master gives talents to his servants, "each according to their ability." He understood that the one-talent man was not capable of producing as much as the five-talent man.

Should we protest this as unfair? Some folks today would say tax the master and the other two and give the one talent guy another shot. That is not what Jesus says in this story. The undeniable truth is that diversity is woven into the very fabric of creation.

The interesting thing about these verses is that while we are not created equal regarding the talents we're given, there is equality found in the Parable of the Talents. The lesson is that it takes just as much work for the five-talent servant to produce five more as it does the two-talent servant to provide two more talents.

Fourth, the Parable of the Talents teaches us that we work for the Master, not our selfish purposes.

We should maximize the use of our talents to honor God, to expand the Kingdom, and to help others. We live and work in a fallen world. Because of the curse of sin, our business will be tough. But deep satisfaction and joy come from doing the best with what God has given us.

Fifth, The Parable of the Talents shows that we will be held accountable. This parable is not about salvation or works of righteousness, but about how we use our work and our business opportunities to fulfill our human callings. It is about whole life stewardship.

The unfaithful servant in this parable didn't so much waste the master's money; he wasted an opportunity. As a result, he was judged as wicked and lazy. You and I are responsible for what we do with the opportunities God brings our way. Don't let fear of failure make you miss an opportunity.

Bible Study Helps

Review the account of the Proverbs 31 woman and choose four character traits you admire about her.

_____

_____

_____

_____

Now, go back and pick three of the traits that you would like to work on beginning today

_____

_____

_____

_____

Review the Parable of the Talents story, paying attention to the five truths discussed in this section of the Bible study and summarize them below.

_____

_____

_____

_____

Now, go back and pick the two that are the most challenging to you and ask the Lord to give you strength to face them and begin to live fearlessly.

_____

_____

_____

_____

Chapter 4
The Fear of Public Speaking

"There are only two types of speakers in the world. 1. The nervous and 2. Liars."[31]
~Mark Twain

If you have a crippling fear of public speaking, recognize that that is perfectly normal. And know that the only way to get over those nerves is to fully understand the material, the points, the policy you are trying to explain - and then practice it a little bit.[32]
~Dana Perino

*F*irst, a point of clarification. Fear of public speaking is real and common. While many love to quote that fear of public speaking is second only to the fear of death, that statistic is grossly overstated. There is very little clinical research that shows the problem to be that severe. When we look at the fear of public speaking we are talking about fear that spans several areas.

In this section, I might sound slightly double-minded. Part of my current professional life is that of a corporate trainer. In this capacity, I have over thirty-five presentations that have been prepared by my company. While I have the ability to infuse my stories and style into the presentations, I am restrained by the content. When I mention things like being familiar with my slide stack, I am referring to the PowerPoints I am required to use.

70

In addition to my corporate job, I do a lot of freelance speaking for business, ministries, and other NGO's [non-governmental agencies]. In that capacity, I can use my passion topics. While there are many things that these two styles of presenting have in common, the latter is the more intimate style. If you are interested in learning more about this style, contact me and I will direct you to a coach or seminar that will be helpful.

Here are some of the reasons people fear public speaking.

1. Self-consciousness in front of large groups. It is the number one reason many individuals feel performance anxiety. I know in my journey as a speaker I've said, "I am fine talking to small groups. But when it is a large crowd of hundreds or thousands, I get wound up." Over the years, I have learned a couple of calculated strategies that have helped me: (1) Remember that the people in a sizable audience are the same ones you talk to individually, and (2) Concentrate on *having a conversation* with your listeners. I promise you will be at your best in every way.

2. Fear of appearing nervous. The prevailing thought is that if you look fearful people will think you do not know your topic. Think back to the last time you saw a speaker appear nervous. What did you think? Probably something like, "Poor him or her! I'd be nervous too." That's what will happen.

3. Concern that others are judging you. Here is a terrible reality: the audience doesn't care about you. They are attending because they came to learn, to get something out of your talk, presentation, or lecture. They hope that their valuable time is well invested while they listen to you. You might also take some comfort with the knowledge that watching a speaker fail is embarrassing for all who are present.

4. Past failures. Public speaking anxiety is often a learned behavior. If you Google "fear of public speaking," you will see many quotes stating it as second only to death, as mentioned earlier. Even though there is no solid clinical research that it is truly that high, the phrase has generated tens of millions of dollars for people who promise to eliminate it.

I have failed at some point in a major speaking situation, and there was a negative seed planted. For a season, I would tell myself I wasn't that good as a speaker. I had a choice at that point: believe the lie, or learn from the setback. I could have wasted the pain of the failure or turned it into an opportunity to grow. Thankfully, I chose the latter. I am grateful for friends and mentors like my wife, Angie; friends like Florence Littauer, Dr. Kevin Leman, LTC David Grossman, who have encouraged me along the way. Plan on succeeding through preparation and practice.

5. Inadequate preparation. One of my seminary professors, Dr. Clyde Fant, used to say, "Always be sure to do proper exegesis on both the Scripture and your audience." **Exegesis** is the critical interpretation of the biblical text to discover its intended meaning. In other words, make sure you know your content and the needs of the audience as well as how to efficiently deliver the goods to them. Nothing will rob public speaking confidence like being unprepared. On the other hand, nothing gives you more confidence than being prepared.

6. Narcissism. This section might be a pill that is a little hard to swallow. In talking with people who have an extreme fear of public speaking, it sometimes seems their concern is selfish. How can you impact your audience if you are entirely wrapped up in your responses? You cannot. So, turn the spotlight around and bring new ideas, clarity, and practical knowledge to your listeners. Remember, it is not about you; it is about the audience.

7. Being discontent with your abilities is one of the legitimate concerns of any speaker. It is also one of the easiest to fix. You should feel dissatisfied if your skills are below par. Get speech training, attend seminars on presentations, hire a speech coach. Just knowing you are developing a great skill set can go a long way in building your confidence. It's also more likely to make you eager to speak.

8. Uneasiness with your own body and movement. I tend to be fidgety, so I move around a lot. I also tend to be a gesticulator, one who moves his hands around a lot. It is one of the ways I burn off nervous energy. Over the years, it was brought to my attention through a couple of mentors that I overdo it sometimes. Did I let that overwhelm me? No. Instead, I invited their counsel. One of them said, "Remember that you are having a conversation with your listeners; it will help you relax. Also, pay attention to how you stand, sit, gesture, and move when you are with friends and family. Then work on recreating your natural movements with larger audiences.

9. **Poor breathing habits.** Unless you have been trained as a singer or actor, there is a good chance you could be unaware of the best method for breathing during a speech. Public speaking requires a lot lung capacity. In addition to taking in breath, your exhaling needs to be more controlled so you can sustain vocalized sounds to the ends of phrases. Belly breathing or diaphragmatic breathing is the key. It is also very helpful in calming your fears. I would encourage you to Google training videos on deep breathing. There is also an outstanding free app called "Tactical Breather." This tool will help you learn how to do relaxation or, as we used to say in the military, range breathing.

10. **Comparing ourselves to others.** Don't dare to compare—it will take you nowhere but down. Your task is to do your job well, pursue the things you are passionate about, and be interesting and engaging when you speak. The truth is that no one can do that as well as you. You are the person your audience came to hear.

※ ※ ※ ※

Now that we have identified some of the common fears of public speaking, let's look at some practical, easy to do steps to overcoming this fear.

Step 1. Reframe the questions you ask yourself. Don't ask, "What will happen if I screw this up?" (which is stinking thinking at its best!) This type of question only leads to catastrophic thinking and bad outcomes. Instead, replace this negative question with a more positive one, such as, "What will happen if I knock it out of the park?" Give this a try; it will calm the noise in your head and give you more confidence as you speak. (You can view more of Seymour's tips in his video "Ask Yourself Good Questions").

Step 2. Practice as if you're the worst. A word of caution: When you know your material well, there's a tendency to get sloppy when practicing a speech. You might flip through your slide stack or your notes, mentally thinking about what you are going to say without actually rehearsing out loud exactly what you plan to say. This can lead to a presentation that's not as sharp as it could be and might cause you to be nervous once you have 100 pairs of eyes staring at you! You can also forget some important sub-points and key soundbites. Know your material, and know where you are and how to get back if you become lost.

Step 3. Familiarize yourself with the sequence of your slide stack or outline. Knowing the sequence of your slides so you can anticipate and announce a slide makes you look in control. (While Keynote and PowerPoint are great tools, way too many people depend on the slides to be the feature of the presentation, not the supporting device it was designed to be). Nothing erodes your credibility faster than having to look at a slide or your notes to know what you have to say next. Being perceived as credible boosts your confidence and reduces your anxiety and the fear of failing.

When I was in seminary at Southwestern Baptist Theological Seminary, one of my preaching professors was Dr. Clyde Fant. Of the many godly men in my life, Dr. Fant was one of the most memorable. In that day, you wrote a complete manuscript and then preached it. Dr. Fant had a somewhat different perspective. He called it an oral script. He taught us that there is no substitute for excellent preparation, but that we should know the material well enough to communicate it clearly. What he called an oral manuscript was an outline with enough meat on the bone to help you make your transitions and emphasize your points.

Step 4. Anticipate questions. One reason people often experience anxiety before a presentation is the fear they'll be asked questions that might be difficult to answer. Don't get caught off guard. Think carefully of what potential issues might arise and rehearse your best answers. Go one step further by creating slides or handouts for some possible questions about complex issues. You can include relevant information in your slide, like your personal contact details, web address, and links to other sites with more information. Remember, it's never bad to say, "I don't know, but I will be glad to get back with you."

Step 5. Visualize your presentation. A study at Harvard University showed the value of visualization in developing a skill. Two groups of volunteers were presented with a piece of unfamiliar piano music. One group was given a keyboard and told to practice. The other group was instructed just to read the music and imagine playing it. When their brain activity was examined, both groups showed expansion in the motor cortex, even though the second group had never touched a keyboard. Visualization is a powerful mental rehearsal tool that peak sports performers use regularly. Einstein said, "Imagination is more important than knowledge." He used visualization throughout his entire life. Take advantage of this tool and visualize yourself successfully delivering your presentation. Concentrate on all the positives of your presentation, and imagine the talk, in detail, from your introduction to your conclusion.

One of the things I routinely do is rehearse in the venue before the crowd arrives. I don't mean just go through your talk, but walk the floor or platform, practice looking at the audience, even though there are only empty chairs in the room. Feel out your space; it will make your delivery much more spontaneous.

You want to imagine people tracking you. You want to see them experience their "lightbulb" moments. You want to see the emails or notes they are going to send you because of the new things they learned from you.

Step 6. Stop seeing your presentation as a performance. Instead, as Jerry Weissman puts it, "Treat every presentation as a series of person-to-person conversations." The more you remind yourself of this, the more you can shift your focus away from the fear-inducing thought that you are required to perform. I personally do this by identifying a few people in the audience and having a conversation with them. If it is a smaller venue, I will go into the audience to make it more intimate and personable.

Step 7. Take some deep breaths. This simple advice cannot be over-emphasized enough. When you're nervous, your breathing is rapid and shallow. This alone can telegraph to the audience that you're not confident. Slow, measured breathing is a sign you're in control. Before you go to the front of the room, concentrate on taking a few slow breaths. Repeat this a few times. When you start to speak, remember to pause and breathe after you make a point. Psychiatrist Fritz Perls said it powerfully: "Fear is excitement without the breath." I use the "Tactical Breather" app to give me both verbal and visual guidance as I do my deep breathing before an event.

Step 8. Try "power posing" before the presentation. Harvard Business School Professor Amy Cuddy discovered that only holding our body in an expansive pose for as little as two minutes results in a higher level of testosterone in our body. Testosterone is the hormone linked to power in both animals and humans. At the same time, the expansive pose lowers our level of cortisol, the stress hormone. In her TED video presentation, Cuddy shows some expansive poses, such as spreading your legs, placing your hands on your hips, or striking the CEO pose: legs resting on a desk, and arms behind your head. You can apply this advice to a presentation to lower your stress level and give yourself a boost. Instead of hunching over your notes or smartphone or iPad, find a spot where you can have some privacy and adopt an expansive pose: Make yourself as big as you can by stretching your arms out and spreading your legs or stand on your tiptoes with your hands in the air.

This stretching limbers you up and helps get more oxygen flowing, plus it "pumps you up."

Step 9. Come to terms with audience expressions. Your level increases when you misinterpret the audience's facial expressions. In normal conversation, we're accustomed to getting feedback from the listener—a nod or a smile here and there that signals approval. But when we present, audiences listen differently. They're more likely to give the speaker a blank stare, which doesn't mean they don't like what they hear; more often than not, it just means they're concentrating on the message. This is particularly the case with audience members who are introverted.

One of the things I do, when possible, is mix and mingle with the attendees before I go on the platform. This way, I already have some friendly faces who will give me feedback. Doing this simple action can be a great way of reducing stress.

Step 10. Attend a speaker training program or get a coach. In an large group or intimate setting you will learn practical, proven techniques, and receive positive coaching and encouragement that will help you become a more effective communicator.

Step 11. Join Toastmasters, and take a speaking class in your community.

Ancient Jewish oral history says, "Because Moses burned his mouth as a child (an act which actually saved his life), he ended up with a slight lisp. In later years when his destiny to confront the king of Egypt was revealed to him by the Almighty, Moses asked, "Why me? I cannot speak well." And yet Moses overcame his fear of speech and made some of the most famous remarks not only to Pharaoh himself but to thousands of ancient Hebrews whom he supported and inspired by his words.

Bible Study Helps

Let's take a brief look at Moses' encounter. You will find it in Exodus 3 and 4—the story of the Burning Bush.

As you read through the story, look for four excuses that Moses offered to the Lord.

#1 Who am I to lead your people?
What was the Lord's response?

_____

#2 Nobody knows who I am.
What was the Lord's response?

_____

#3 What if they don't believe me?

What was the Lord's response? (Hint, it had to do with something in his hand)

_____

#4 I am scared!

What was the Lord's response?

_____

Chapter 5
The Fear of Rejection

Your weaknesses and struggles are not reasons for him to give up on you. Instead, they're opportunities for you to show his strength in ways you simply can't on your best days.[33]
~Holley Gerth

One of the major things that can slow people in the direct service/ sales industry, or any other endeavor, is the fear of rejection. This fear is a dream stealer and an income robber.

What is the fear of rejection?

The fear of rejection is a powerful fear that can cast a long shadow over a person's life. Most of us experience the same fear and anxiety when placed in situations that could lead to rejection, but for some people, the fear can become debilitating. An untreated fear of rejection tends to worsen over time, gradually consuming every part of an individual's life.

Common Behaviors Associated with those Who have a Fear of Rejection.

Phoniness: Many people who are afraid of rejection develop a carefully choreographed life. Fearing rejection, people will often live behind a mask. This type of angst can make an individual seem bogus and counterfeit to others and could cause a rigid unwillingness to learn from life's challenges.

People pleasing: While it is entirely reasonable to take care of the people we love, those who fear rejection often go overboard. They may find it impossible to say no, even though it might be an inconvenience, or cause a significant hardship. This type of people pleasing can lead to burnout. Worst case: People pleasing behaviors can turn into enabling the wrong actions of others.

Unassertiveness: Many individuals who fear rejection go out of their way to avoid confrontations. They refuse to ask for what they want or need. A common tendency for individuals who struggle with fear of rejection is to simply shoot down their needs or pretend their needs do not matter.

Passive aggressiveness: Uncomfortable showing off their true selves but unable to entirely shut down their needs, many people who fear rejection behave in passive aggressive ways. They might "forget" to keep promises, complain, and work inefficiently on projects they take on.

Additionally, the fear of rejection often restrains a person from going after their dreams. Putting yourself out there is a frightening experience for anyone, but if you have a fear of rejection, you may feel immobilized, frozen in place. You may feel safer staying in the harbor than leaving for the open sea. If a person chooses to give in to the fear of rejection, it will stop them from approaching their full potential.

As the fear of rejection spins its web around you, it can lead to behaviors that make you seem insecure, ineffective, and overwhelmed. You might sweat, shake, fight, avoid eye contact, and even lose the ability to effectively communicate. While people react to these behaviors in a broad variety of ways, below are some of the common reactions.

Rejection: Ironically, the fear of rejection often becomes a self-fulfilling prophecy. A 2009 study at the University of Florida demonstrated that confidence is nearly as important as intelligence in determining our income level! As a rule of thumb, the lack of self-confidence connected to the fear of rejection makes an individual more likely to be rejected.

Manipulation: Some corrupt people prey on the insecurity of others. Those who experience fear of rejection could be at a high risk of being manipulated for someone else's personal gain.

Frustration: Most people in this world are decent, honest, and straightforward. Rather than manipulating someone with the fear of rejection, they will try to help. Be intentional about looking for signs that your family and friends are trying to encourage your assertiveness, asking you to be more open with them, or probing for your real feelings. Unfortunately, however, people who fear rejection see these attempts to help as signs of possible future rejection. This dread can often lead friends and family to "walk on eggshells," fearful of making fears worse. Over time, family and friends may become frustrated and angry. They may either confront you about your behaviors or begin to distance themselves from you.

When was the last time you felt a sense of rejection creeping up on you? Maybe you went through a rough patch with your friends or received negative feedback from a client or customer. Whether it is your personal or professional life, rejection can and will happen to everyone at some point, and more than once. As hard as it might be to hear or to put what you are feeling into perspective at the time, being rejected offers you the opportunity to reflect and learn something new about yourself.

When it comes to rejection, many of us blame themselves or others immediately.

Regardless of your background or gender, how you handle rejection is much more important than the rejection itself. Here are four techniques to handle rejection:

1. Take a step back and assess the circumstances. Rejection may have little to do with it. Sometimes the situation may be completely out of your ability to control it. Many times, rejection isn't at all about you. It's the rejection of an idea, a course of direction, a wounded place in the person dishing out the rejection, etc.

2. Create an active support system. A crucial piece of managing rejection is to have a strong support team to lean on. It is a cake-walk to lean on your support system when things are going well, but when times are tough, you need this group more than ever. Who do you turn to when you need support? Whether friends, a mentor, a supportive coworker, or a life partner, it is important to have a group of people who will never let you throw in the towel and give up.

3. Believe in your dream, your "why."

4. Think about this tongue-in-cheek theological issue: "God don't make any junk!"

We all feel the sting of rejection at some point in our lives. When it happens, we always have two options: We can give into defeat or turn it into an opportunity for learning and growth.

The choice is yours. Choose wisely.

Emma is a stay at home mom who recently began a home-based business. She'd started her business with her husband's full support. Emma was off to a great start. She'd had several successful jewelry shows, had earned her initial investment back the first month, and had sponsored two of her friends. She was excited, as was Cody, her husband. Recently she'd taken Cody to his favorite restaurant and treated him to an excellent steak dinner.

She felt motivated, fulfilled and blessed. She was becoming a young, confident leader. Then her mom called.

Emma and her mom had been alienated for years. Emma told me her mom was one of the most conservative, mean women she'd ever known. Her mom had made a choice to climb the corporate ladder. In the wake of her decision, she and her husband had divorced and a nanny had raised Emma and her sister. Her mom had crashed through the glass ceiling in her company, but at terrific cost.

Emma had never felt much of her mom's love. As a case in point, when she married Cody, Emma's mother said she thought she could do better. Cody worked as a teacher and a coach at the local high school, a job he loved. Emma constantly felt the pressure of her mom's unrealistic expectations and made a choice to disengage from the toxicity of her mother's negativity.

It was about three o'clock one afternoon when the phone rang. It was Emma's mom, "Well, what's this I hear about you starting a jewelry business? My friend Nancy told me her daughter was doing one of the home show things. Are things so bad that you're going to be a jewelry lady? After all the money I spent on your education, you want to be a stay home mom. I had hoped for so much more."

Suddenly, like a fast-growing kudzu vine, Emma was feeling suffocated by the old, familiar chokehold of the rejection from her childhood.

She felt her confidence leak out faster than the air from a bicycle tire with a goat head in it. She listened to her mom's rant for a couple more minutes until she heard her little girl crying as she awoke from her afternoon nap. Her baby's tears delivered her from her mother's rejection.

For the next hour, she tightly held on to Gracie, telling her how much she loved her. She cried; she felt angry, hurt, completely disrespected, and disregarded by her mom.

Those old familiar feelings were back on her like a thick, wet, musty wool blanket.

For the next few days, she circled the wagons. She told Cody what had happened, and Cody gave her space she needed.

As he held close, he encouraged her to remember the things she'd learned during her time with her Christian counselor. Emma looked at Cody, gave him a tender kiss and went to her home office.

For a while she prayed, cried, and beat an overstuffed pillow like it was a side of beef from a Rocky movie. As she began to settle down, she pulled out her journal and began to review what she'd learned over the years.

The first thing she considered were the four ways she used to reject herself. Her counselor had given her a handout that was helpful:

1. **Judging yourself**. Do you feel rejected when others judge or reject you? The same things happen on the inside. When others reject or judge us, we in turn judge ourselves—a shared and dominant form of self-rejection.

Are you aware of how you feel when you begin to go down the negative path? Or have you learned to "numb out," which is a very common form of self-rejection? Are you aware that when you turn on yourself, you are more likely to feel anxious, depressed, guilty, shamed, and angry?

2. **Ignoring your feelings by staying in your mind**. One of the ways many of us learn not to feel our pain is to disconnect from our body, where our feelings are, and focus on our mind instead. The problem occurs that when we stay in our mind and disconnect from all our emotions, we deny a crucial part of how God designed us.

Here is an essential point that is so simple it's easily missed. *Stop Rehearsing the Hurts*. If you have boys, I know you've said things like,

"If you keep picking that scab, it will not heal!" The same truth applies to our emotional scars.

3. Turning to addictions to avoid feeling your feelings. Did you learn to use food, sex, alcohol, drugs, TV, or the internet to avoid your feelings? How much time do you spend on Pinterest or Facebook?

The brain is a funny thing. You might think you are rewarding yourself when turning to addictive behaviors, but whenever you ignore those feelings in any way, you will feel the anxiety, fear, depression, guilt, shame, anger, and self-loathing that comes from self-rejection. Then, to avoid these added feelings, you reject yourself more with your self-judgments, or by ignoring your feelings, staying in your mind, and turning to your addictions.

4. Making others responsible for your feelings. Did you grow up believing that others are responsible for making you feel safe and worthy? While our parents were responsible for us when we were kids, as adults it is up to us to give ourselves the loving attention and approval we need to feel lovable and worthy. We are also responsible to learn to receive and apply God's love.

Did you learn to give yourself up, or get angry at others, in an attempt to get love and avoid responsibility for your feelings?

As Emma reviewed and remembered the personal work she had done in therapy, combined with helpful, regular Bible study, she began to re-engage her brain and come up with five things she could do to overcome the rejection:

1. She remembered there's nothing to fear but fear itself.

2. She recalled how we always have two choices.

Give in to the fear; give up, quit, or . . .

Embrace the fear and turn it into an opportunity for growth and increased understanding.

Her therapist taught her to "walk circumspectly," a biblical term that means to be aware of what's going on around you (Ephesians 5:15 NLT). For her, it meant being aware of the types of things that trigger her in a negative way.

3. She began to use her imagination and memories of fun times she had building her business. As she exercised this new behavior, she started to feel an energy source.

4. She remembered words from one of my speaking events—*Nothing stays in your head rent-free. It is something that will either build you or hold you back.*

5. Kelly Clarkston's "What doesn't kill you makes you stronger/ What doesn't kill you makes you a fighter" rang true. Emma pulled out her phone and went to her playlist and selected that song to remind her that she was on overcomer.

Action Plan

Go back and review the five things that you can do to push back the fear of rejection and jot them down.

_____
_____
_____
_____

Now, pick two of these action items that you are going to use to help you deal with the fear of rejections.

_____
_____
_____
_____

Bible Study Helps
Memorize and reflect on this verse from Isaiah 41:10:

*Don't be afraid, for I am with you. Don't be
discouraged, for I am your God.
I will strengthen you and help you. I will hold y
ou up with my victorious right hand.* (NLT)

Even in our fear, the Lord promises to do what?

_____

_____

_____

_____

Chapter 6
The Fear of Success

The fear of success is easy to miss because it looks a lot like garden-variety procrastination and insecurity.[34]
~Jeneka

Are you allowing the fear of success to steal your hope, your life, and your dream day by day?

The Unknown, Possibly America's Best Photographer

The following story, by James Clear, compelled me to take some new steps in my own life.[35]

It was 2007 and John Maloof was working on a book about Chicago's northwest neighborhoods. One day, he searched for photographs from the 1960s that he could use in his book.

What he found was far more attractive.

After buying a box of negatives from a local auction house, he began developing some of the images. When he finished processing them, he was stunned at the quality of the photographs. The box produced more than 3,000 images. Whoever had taken these pictures was surely one of the most prolific and talented American photographers in the past hundred years.

And yet when Maloof researched the photographer's name, he could not find her work anywhere. After further studies, Maloof was reasonably sure nobody had ever heard of this woman. Her obituary never mentioned she was a photographer. She was a mystery, an unknown artist, with world class talent.

These powerful images were taken by a nanny named Vivian Maier. (If you would like to view some of her incredible images, go to www.vivianmaier.com).

For close to forty years, Maier worked as a nanny for wealthy families in Chicago and New York. Maier took nearly 150,000 photographs of the people and architecture that surrounded her.

The uncovering of this treasure has been referred to as one of the greatest photographic discoveries of the 21st Century.

This enticing story raises plenty of questions, not just about Maier's past, but also about our desire to share our gifts with the world.

Clear goes on to say, "We'll never know the reason why Vivian Maier decided to hide her work away in boxes (like a lamp under a basket). Maybe she didn't feel they were good enough. Maybe she wanted to share them but didn't know who to contact. Maybe she only loved to create and wanted to keep her work private. (This seems unlikely as she had made an attempt to publish her work.)"[36]

The following is an insightful view of success from a biblical perspective provided by Fred Smith:

Before we go any further, let's define *success*. Many people have the wrong understanding of it.

> *For Christians, success can never be measured by money. When people say to me, "That man's worth ten million dollars," that tells me he's wealthy, but it doesn't prove he's successful. In some cases, it could mean the opposite. For instance, if Mother Teresa, whom I consider a tremendous success, confessed she was hoarding a million dollars, I'd think she was a hypocrite. The money would prove her a fraud, not a success.*

> *The measurement of success is simply the ratio of talents used to talents received: What you are doing with what you've got, plus who you are becoming. Are you a growing, maturing Christian? Whether you work in business or in Christian work, or as a day laborer, professional, or academic, if you are a growing Christian using a significant percentage of your talents, you are successful. Be glad.* [37]

One of the major differences between people who are fruitful and those who are unfruitful is that successful, forward-looking people get excited about any small step of progress they make toward a goal. Any little win or small victory seems to fire them up and push them toward their goals and dreams.

Yet, people who fear success focus on their lack of success. Any slip-up or misstep seems to fuel their fear of success. They read the blackmail of fear which says something like, "You will never measure up." This leads them to think, "See, I cannot do this, I am hopeless, I will never amount to anything." As a result, they lay their life, hope, and dreams on the altar of fear.

While this may seem odd to many, it is a form of self-sabotage that can make things fearful. From getting hired, messing up a relationship, or missing opportunities that come your way, we can sabotage our plans.

To kill fear, you must identify it, call it by its name, and cut off its fuel source. Rather than passively feeding the fear, you need to get crystal clear about the dream God has given you and make sure you are adding fuel to the fire of your dream!

The fear of success is very much like the fear of failure. Both prevent the individual from achieving their dreams and goals. Many people get so accustomed to this mindset that they convince themselves it is okay to never think about getting ahead in life.

Here are a few of the behaviors of Success-Fearing People:

- You do not complete your projects at home or at work.
- You talk about what you're going to do more than what you actually do.
- You work as a chicken with its head cut off on several projects at once, not really
- focusing intensely on any of them.
- Your vision board has the exact same things on it that it did three years ago.
- The one consistent thing you do is second-guess yourself.
- Distraction is your middle name.

- You don't think your work is ever quite good enough.
- And the BIG giveaway – you are on the verge of "success," and things start going really wrong.

If this sounds like you, I bet you are asking, "What can I do about fear of success?"

The above list represents the classic symptoms of someone who struggles with the fear of success. It's not that you don't want to be successful, because you have probably been working your tail off and spent many a night thinking, dreaming, and strategizing. The truth is, if success doesn't come quickly to you, on an individual level you might not want to succeed or feel you deserve to. These thoughts hide in your subconscious mind and, over time, may have been put there through a variety of life experiences.

The fear of appearing to be unspiritual. Christians seem to be more prone to this fear than most people. Christian teaching often fails to balance biblical perspectives on the evils of the desires of the flesh and the need for self-denial, with the positive role of motivation and accomplishment in the Christian life. The end result is many success "phobics" among modern Christians. Many believe God does not want them to enjoy significant success.

This idea is rampant in many faith communities. I will typically hear the verse, "It's easier for a camel to go through the eye of a needle than for a rich man to enter the Kingdom of Heaven." I also hear, "Rich people are greedy," or, "It is better to give than to receive." These are very common thoughts and sayings that tend to bubble up in our thought processes directly related to the phrase "feeling unspiritual." On a personal note, I have had to work on this one myself.

There appear to be more nobility and humility in failure and much less hazard to your relationship with the Lord. Is this true?

The Word of God offers plenty of warning about trusting in riches and the dangers of success. Yet is speaks just as often about the positive side of success and the importance of using our gifts, resources, and mind constructively for God's glory. Psalms 1:3 (NLT) says, "They are like trees planted along the riverbank, bearing fruit each season. Their leaves never wither, and they prosper in all they do." The Lord has ordained each of our lives for certain accomplishments. Yet the fear of success can and will hold us back.

The Fisherman's Story

> One day as Jesus was preaching on the shore of the Sea of Galilee, great crowds pressed in on him to listen to the word of God. He noticed two empty boats at the water's edge, for the fishermen had left them and were washing their nets. Stepping into one of the boats, Jesus asked Simon, its owner, to push it out into the water. So he sat in the boat and taught the crowds from there. When he had finished speaking, he said to Simon, "Now go out where it is deeper, and let down your nets to catch some fish."
>
> "Master," Simon replied, "we worked hard all last night and didn't catch a thing. But if you say so, I'll let the nets down again." And this time, their nets were so full of fish they began to tear! A shout for help brought their partners in the other boat, and soon both boats were filled with fish and on the verge of sinking. Luke 5:1-11 (NLT)

Looking at these verses with a fresh set of eyes, I can see it as one example of the fear of success. Simon and his friends were career fishermen. They had been fishing all night and caught nothing. Jesus tells them to drop their nets once again, and this time, their catch is so big they can barely haul the catch ashore. Peter then says to Jesus, "Depart from me, for I am a sinful man, Lord."

I don't know about you, but I think if I had been one of those fishermen, I would have been overjoyed at such a huge catch. I would surely want Jesus to hang around and bring us more success.

Instead, they were completely blown away and thrown off-guard by this miracle. They had grown accustomed to failure, and success was a shock to their comfort zone. They felt utterly unworthy of it. They undoubtedly feared that as Jesus came to know them deeper and better, He would judge them as posers and use this same miraculous power to destroy them.

Jesus, being full of mercy and grace, ignored Peter's self-defeating request. (Thank the Lord, He often ignores our misguided attempts at prayer.) He assured Peter and his friends that He intended much more success for them, on a more significant level.

When Simon Peter realized what had happened, he fell to his knees before Jesus and said, "Oh, Lord, please leave me—I'm such a sinful man." He was awestruck by the number of fish they had caught, as were the others with him. His partners, James and John, the sons of Zebedee, were also amazed.

They were so relieved to discover Jesus had positive intentions for them that "they pulled their boats up on the shore, left everything and followed him."

Our relationship with money and spirituality has always been complicated. Money is more like a symbol for what we want, what we don't want, what we can get, what we can't get, where we go on vacation or not go, what we'd give away, and what we'd hold on tightly to. Money has a tightly woven and complicated relationship with our integrity.

Here is the error in our thinking: Someone with money helped fund Jesus's ministry. Paul was sometimes supported by others with money. Churches and ministries get generous gifts and other contributions— that is what keeps them going. If it were not for productive, godly people, many ministries and churches would not exist.

Action Plan

Reality check and news flash: Not everyone is going to like you whether you are broke or wealthy. Accept it. No matter how good you are or how kind you think you are, most people could care less. Instead, a more biblical view is to focus on who you want to serve and why, whether to you family, in your business, church, or community.

Work on becoming crystal clear about what you are willing to give of yourself. Tithing is a spiritual practice that many successful people follow. It involves donating a percentage of your income— traditionally 10%--back to a religious organization or charity. You can also tithe your time and energy to serving others without a desire for anything in return.

Fear of standing out. The fear of standing out can bring you to your knees. In the past, I had a ton of brilliant ideas that would have helped me stand out more online, but I didn't execute them. Do you know why? I told myself it was because I didn't want the attention. Or all the hard work was not worth the effort.

The biggest truth was that I was afraid to be extraordinary. Blending in with the crowd is easy. It means not dealing with rejection or worrying about the possibility of making someone else feel inadequate.

What to do:

This is a quote adapted from Marianne Williamson. Read through it a couple of times and reflect on what it is saying to you.

> *Our deepest fear is not that we are inadequate. Our deepest fear is that we are powerful beyond measure. It is our light, not our darkness that most frightens us. We ask ourselves, Who am I to be brilliant, gorgeous, talented, fabulous? Actually, who are you not to be? You are a child of God. Your playing small does not serve the world. There is nothing enlightened about shrinking so that other people won't feel insecure around you. We are all meant to shine.*

Now read this from the Gospel of Matthew:

> *You are the light of the world—like a city on a hilltop that cannot be hidden. No one lights a lamp and then puts it under a basket. Instead, a lamp is placed on a stand, where it gives light to everyone in the house. In the same way, let your good deeds shine out for all to see so that everyone will praise your heavenly Father.* Matthew 5:14-16 (NLT)

We were born to make manifest the glory of God within us. It's not just in some of us; it's for everyone. And as we let our own light shine, we unconsciously give other people permission to do the same. As we are liberated from our own fear, our presence automatically liberates others.

The Fear of Change. For the past 33 years, I have looked in the mirror every morning and asked myself: "If today were the last day of my life, would I want to do what I am about to do today? And whenever the answer has been "No" for too many days in a row, I've known I need to change something." Steve Jobs[38]

Failure to adjust to changes that come your way can have a negative impact in at least seven areas of your life.

1. Physical Health. Imagine carrying around a stone that represents the negative impact of fear on your physical health. That fifty-pound stone affects your physical health. Residual anxiety, stress, and worry can cause headaches, muscle pain, chest pains, insomnia, and a suppressed immune system.

2. Psychological Health. That rock can increase the risk of needless worry, anxiety, depression, and general well-being. Failure to make the changes and adjustments you need to make will consume more energy and distraction than the actual change itself.

3. Relationships. If the changes you are avoiding have to do with your relationships, what is that costing you? Are you settling for "comfortable" at the cost of having a healthy relationship?

4. Work. Is staying in the maintaining mode of your business making you money? Is failure to expand preventing you from growing? The Laws of the Universe indicate that if you're not growing, you are decaying.

5. Fun. Maybe you've been avoiding fun. Research shows that having a good time promotes happiness. Positive Psychology studies show that this is a must in having a workplace that is safe, productive, and profitable.

6. Finance. Failure to change in the area of economics may very well impact a lack of financial growth in your personal and professional life.

7. Spirituality. It's difficult to be true to yourself, to apply your values, strengths, and faith when you are under the pressure that comes with resisting change.

When we are not living the life God desires, we often behave in unhealthy ways; overspending, addictive behaviors, and other harmful practices.

When you decide to make needed changes, there is a shift in your thinking and in your energy. When you use your faith to take the step, you are rewarded with the strength and joy that enables you to follow through with those changes.

Change is a natural, organic part of life. Nothing really stays the same, but the thing is, it can *feel* like it does. Especially, when it comes to the ins and outs of your life from day to day.

Success, by its very nature, means you now will be tasked with or experience something different—something you didn't have before. And the Catch-22 is that we really want this change on one level, but on another level, it could be a very frightening thought!

When we fail to achieve a goal, we know what to expect. We're already used to living the way we do. On the other hand, success can be scary because it brings uncharted territory. Imagine if you've been overweight your whole life. What might it be like to be slim for the first time ever? It's a new, slim you. How will a *slim you* dress? How will a *slim you* behave? Who will a *slim you* hang out with—new friends from the gym?

What about creating a business that brings in so much money that it's easy to share and give to others. Yikes! You spend so much of your time juggling bills right now. Can you even imagine what new habits you might have if you were rich? Would you suddenly be more wasteful? Would your children be ungrateful?

What about a relationship starting or ending? Or moving?

Change can be amazing or frustrating or liberating or scary. Quite often it's tedious, character-building work. It's also inevitable, so we should probably choose what we *really* want!

What to do:

If change is inevitable (and it is), then the first thing to do is begin the process of getting absolutely clear on what you want. Write a description of the life you really want, without judgment. Just let it pour out onto the paper.

Next, gather a great support system around you. This could be sharing your vision of your life with someone you love and trust, joining a Facebook group of people who are going for the same goal, investing in a mentor, or reading an excellent book that resonates with the description of the life you really want.

So, Now What?

Now breathe. Deeply. Success comes in stages. You'll always have the capacity to improve and strive for yet another success. When you're done breathing, look at the thing you want most right now. Break it down and focus on two things you can do today. And then just be the unique person that God designed you to be.

Bible Study Helps

A key part of God's design is to create and bring increase. These are vital factors to understand as you build your business.

From a faith perspective, success is not measured in fame, money, prestige, or how many toys you have. It is measured by how many lives you touch.

These can be lives you touched personally, through the profits of your business, the developing of your gifts, talents, and temperament.

As we move into the action chapter here are some closing thoughts about biblical success:

It is rooted in the art and hard work of **diligence**.

> *Work hard and become a leader; be lazy and become a slave.* Proverbs 12:24 (NLT)

Become a person of **excellence**.
> *Do you see any truly competent workers? They will serve kings rather than working for ordinary people.* Proverbs 22:29 (NLT)

Assume responsibility and manage details.
> *Know the state of your flocks, and put your heart into caring for your herds.* Proverbs 27:23 (NLT)

Strive for trustworthiness and dependability.

Who may worship in your sanctuary, Lord?
Who may enter the presence of your holy hill?
Those who lead blameless lives and do what is right,
speaking the truth from sincere hearts.
Those who refuse to gossip or harm their neighbors or speak
evil of their friends. Psalms 15:1-4 (NLT)

Treat your customer like family.

Choose a good reputation over great riches;
being held in high esteem is better than silver or gold.
True humility and fear of the Lord lead to riches, honor,
and long life. Proverbs 22: 1,4 (NLT)

Develop a long-term perspective.

Do your planning and prepare your fields before building
your house. Proverbs 24:27 (NLT)

Be alert for opportunities to expand your business.

She goes to inspect a field and buys it; with her earnings
she plants a vineyard. Proverbs 31: 16

Manage risk well.

Even when there was no reason for hope, Abraham kept
hoping—believing that he would become the father of
many nations. For God had said to him, "That's how
many descendants you will have! Romans 4:18

Make your assets work for you.

Well done, my good and faithful servant. You have been
faithful in handling this small amount, so now I will give
you many more responsibilities. Let's celebrate together!
Matthew 25:21 (NLT)

Surround yourself with wise counselors.

Without wise leadership, a nation falls; there is safety in
having many advisers. Proverbs 11:14 (NLT)

Make decisions based on biblical principles.

O people, the Lord has told you what is good, and this is what he requires of you: to do what is right, to love mercy, and to walk humbly with your God. Micah 6:8 (NLT)

Ask the Lord Jesus to be your CEO.

Seek the Kingdom of God[a] above all else, and live righteously, and he will give you everything you need. Matthew 6:33 (NLT)

Chapter 7
Next Steps

*You just don't luck into things as much as you'd like
to think you do. You build step by step, whether it's
friendships or opportunities.* [39]
~Barbara Bush

*God has equipped you to handle difficult things. In fact,
He has already planted the seeds of discipline and self-
control inside you. You just have to water those seeds with
His Word to make them grow!*[40]
~Joyce Meyer

I have attempted to give you practical, researched information to help
you succeed in your business endeavors. The next decision you make
is completely up to you. You can choose to do nothing, or you can
embrace personal responsibility and trust the Lord to lead you into the
truth. It is not an easy process but is a simple one.

I began my relationship with Christ over forty-five years ago.
Within about a month of discovering my new-found faith, a friend
suggested I start a daily devotional. The plan was simple, but it has had
a powerful impact on my life, even to this day. Want to know what it
is?

Here it is. Read a Proverb a day. In the English Bible, there are 31
chapters in the book of Proverbs, all but two chapters are attributed to
King Solomon. Personally, I have read through the Book of Proverbs
more times than I can count, and each time I have gained new and fresh

insight into relationships, integrity, character building, intentionality, diligence, and lessons on success.

Solomon was born around 974 B.C. and was installed as King of Israel by his father, David, shortly before David died. At the time, Solomon was twelve years old. He was scared of ruling Israel, fearful that he didn't have the wisdom to do so. Based on the account in the Old Testament, God appeared to Solomon and asked him what he wanted. The young king asked only for wisdom and knowledge so he could rightly judge the great people of the nation of Israel (1 Kings 3:9; 11 Chronicles 1:10). God then told him that because he did not ask for riches, wealth, and honor, the life of his enemies, nor a longer life for himself, He would give Solomon more wisdom, knowledge, riches, wealth and honor than any king before him or any king who would follow him. What was promised was delivered. Solomon's wisdom, success, and wealth increased beyond imagination. In addition to his gold reserves, he owned 4,000 stalls for his horses and chariots.

My wife Angie and I were able to visit some of the stalls on a trip to Israel in 2014. Solomon was not only known for his wealth, but also for his wisdom. Rulers of nations throughout the world sought his advice and paid dearly for it. In the interest of complete disclosure, Solomon was by no means a perfect man. By the middle of his life, he began to violate the very laws of living he had so brilliantly articulated in the Book of Proverbs. As he did, his success and happiness evaporated. Imagine the impact if he had stayed faithful to those laws for living, those wisdom words He'd received from God!

One of the several themes even a casual reader of the Book of Proverbs will catch is the concept of diligence or intentionality. Long before any psychologist, life coach, or mental health professional thought about living an intentional life, King Solomon had written about it.

Here are a couple of definitions that will help you grasp the concept.

Intentional means deliberate, calculated, intended, conscious, willful, or purposeful.

Diligence is a learnable skill that combines creative persistence; a smart-working effort properly planned and rightly performed in a timely, efficient, and effective manner to attain a result that is pure and of the highest quality of excellence.[41]

Have you ever noticed how we as humans are always looking for the path of least resistance, the shortcut, or the cheat sheet? Solomon rightly understood that we need to be motivated to choose diligence and intentionality over our natural tendency to "go with the flow." And what is motivation? Being truly diligent, he tells us, brings valuable rewards, while a lack of diligence can have devastating consequences.

The focus of this book is getting a grip on fear. While the previous chapters have identified at least six of the common concerns, as well as some proven, practical tips to overcome the fear, the real key to overcoming these fears involves focused, deliberate work.

Here are some key elements lifted from the Book of Proverbs. I hope you will strongly consider using them as you push back unproductive fear.

You will gain an advantage others do not have.

In anything, would you rather have a substantial advantage or a permanent handicap? King Solomon assures us that those who are diligent will gain an insurmountable advantage over those who are not. He says, "The plans of the diligent lead surely to advantage." (Proverbs 21:5). Applying this to our fears means we can learn to turn our fears away from things that steal our energy into thoughts that can propel us forward.

You will be in control of the situation (fear), rather than have the situation (fear) control you.

It comes right back to the choices you and I make. The key question is, would you prefer to have your life controlled by fear, or would you rather monitor and manage your fear and make it work for you? Solomon says, "The hand of the diligent will rule, but the slack hand will be put to forced labor." (Proverbs 12:24, AMP). Those who are truly careful not only control their destiny but enhance the achievements of those around them as well.

You will experience true fulfillment.

Have you ever noticed how hungry Americans are for things? Americans today have more debt and fewer savings than any other generation in our nation's history. No matter what we have, it never seems to be enough. Contentment and a sense of real fulfillment seem to be about as rare as a winning lotto ticket. In stark contrast, Solomon tells us, "The appetite of the diligent is abundantly supplied." (Proverbs 13:4 AMP). The word appetite can mean our innermost being, our core, the seat of our emotions and personality. Can you imagine what it would feel like to be so content and fulfilled that you craved nothing? This feeling is the kind of fulfillment that can result from intentionality and diligence.

You will attain the respect and admiration of those in authority.

While others fight to be noticed, the diligent are sought out to be people in positions of power or prominence. That is what Solomon means when he says the individual who is diligent "will stand before kings" (Proverbs 22:29).

Your needs will be satisfied.

Those who work diligently to deal with life's issues and their chosen field of expertise will achieve enough material success to satisfy their needs. In Proverbs 28:19, Solomon writes, "He that tills his land shall be satisfied but he who follows vain persons is void of understanding." If you stray from your field of endeavors, like building your business or listening to fear, to follow vain people or their advice, you will lose your path to understanding. Thurman's modern translation, "Don't be deceived by individuals who look successful on the surface and offer 'get rich quick schemes' that sound too good to be true. They are. In the words of Jenny in the movie, *Forest Gump,* "Run, Forest, Run!"

You will experience ever-increasing success.

Solomon assures us that those who diligently labor will experience success and wealth will continually grow, but money that comes to us easily, without significant effort, will nearly always be lost. In applying this principle to pushing back fear, as you learn the principles of defeating fear, you will experience increased joy and confidence. Proverbs 13:11 (NLT) says, "Wealth from get-rich quick schemes quickly disappears; wealth from hard work grows over time."

Your efforts will be profitable.

Solomon promises that all diligent labor results in profit that can be measured by the successful achievement of your goals, and the financial rewards you receive for achieving those goals. This principle can be readily applied to pushing back fear. In Proverbs 14:23 (NLT), he says, "In all labor there is profit, but mere talk leads to poverty." If you apply that energy to your marriage, parenting, overcoming fear, building your business, or your spiritual pilgrimage, your profit will be measured by the amount of fulfillment you and your family will gain. On the other hand, mere talk, Solomon warns, is cheap and easy, and only leads to poverty. Diligent, intentional effort is demanding. It requires effort, vision, creativity, commitment, fellow travelers, and active partnering. Solomon is telling us that if you are not profitable in your career, having trouble managing fear, or your relationships are not as fulfilling as you wish, you are probably not working diligently enough. Applying diligence and intentionality to any area of our lives always brings favorable results.

So What Happens If You Fail to be Diligent and Intentional?

Our greatest motivations in life are the desire for gain and the fear of loss. Solomon attempts to motivate us with both. If his seven rewards don't provide the motivation you need to pursue diligence and intentionality, perhaps the consequences of not being diligent will give you a reality check.

You will always be at an insurmountable disadvantage.

The hard-working, intentional person puts in the time to plan and prepare so they can perform with excellence. Those who are not diligent and fail to prepare, plan, or perform will either experience an arduous journey or fail to achieve what they set out to do. Solomon says, "The plans of the diligent lead surely to advantage. But everyone who is hasty (comes) surely to poverty," Proverbs 21:5 NLT.

You will be ruled.

I do not know anyone who likes living a life that feels out of control. We hate being controlled by others, by events, and by fears. Solomon warns, "The hand of the diligent will rule, but the slack hand will be put to forced labor," Proverbs 12:24 KJV. If you want to keep fear, anxiety, and worry away, then you have to do the work.

Solomon's Steps to Bring Diligence and Intentionality into Your Life.

Being diligent and intentional requires time and effort. The good news is that it will bring about amazing results. Solomon gives us four steps we can use to increase diligence and intentionality:

Step # 1 – Wake up and Smell the Coffee

"But you, lazybones, how long will you sleep? When will you wake up? A little extra sleep, a little more slumber, a little folding of the hands to rest—then poverty will pounce on you like a bandit; scarcity will attack you like an armed robber," Proverbs 6:9-11 NLT

Don't be asleep to the realities around you. If you fail to deal with fear, it will deal with you. It will rob you, steal your joy, and remove opportunity. The clock is ticking, and we are not guaranteed tomorrow. That is why it is so important to deal with the fear, anxiety, stress, and worry that is holding you back. Wake up and realize you can bring intentionality and diligence into your life. As you take the powerful, faith-filled steps to push back fear and get in the game, your opportunities will be multiplied. Assume responsibility for your life, your attitudes, your values, and how you spend your time.

Step #2 – Define Your Visions

Solomon hit the nail on the head in Proverbs 28:19: "Without a vision, the people perish." Another way to look at this verse is this: Where there is no vision, we lose our direction, our motivation, our joy, our passion, our energy, our creativity, and our commitment. Thankfully, the opposite is true. Whenever you bring new vision into your life, you gain new energy, insight, and a refreshed sense of purpose.

Whether you are building a business, starting a ministry, or learning new ways to overcome fear, stress, anxiety, and worry, you will discover direction, motivation, strength, joy, passion, peace, and creativity. Defining and clarifying your vision is a fundamental component in developing diligence and intentionality. Bringing these two powerful forces into your life will be a huge blessing. In Proverbs 6:6-7 Solomon tells those who lack diligence to look at the ant, which "have no prince or governor or ruler to make them work, they labor hard all summer, gathering food for the winter." NLT In other words, the ant is so mission-focused that even without any external controls, it does what it needs to do for its benefit and the benefit of the colony.

Step # 3- Effectively Partner

"Plans go wrong for lack of advice, many advisers bring success." Proverbs 15:22 NLT

When looking at partnering, I am referring to the help of advisors, counselors, other successful people, mentors, and anyone else who can provide you with the knowledge and skills needed to achieve your mission.

Step # 4 – Pursue Wisdom; Build Your Life Upon it

"How much better it is to get wisdom than gold! And to get understanding is to be chosen above silver," Proverbs 16:16 NLT.

The final component critical to becoming an intentional, diligent person is to pursue wisdom and build your life upon its foundation. Solomon tells us to seek wisdom as if it were a hidden treasure. True wisdom is rarely found lying on the ground in plain view. Rather, it is a treasure that must be searched out, and those seeking it must often dig for it.

Joan Horner, the co-founder of Premier Designs Jewelry, and a friend who passed away in 2010 put it this way:

Work for what you believe in. My precious friend Mary Crowley used to quote a little rhyme:

> *If you work for the thing you believe in,*
> *You're rich though the way be rough.*
> *If you are working only for money,*
> *You can never earn quite enough.* [42]

She believed this. She's a marvelous example of one who fell in love with hard work, with the enjoyment of it and the accomplishments of it. "Find something to do that you love to do so much, you will do it for free. Then learn to be so good at it that the world pays you well to do it." Through hard work—Mary built a multi-million dollar company on this premise.

In Proverbs 14:23 (NLT) we read, "Work brings profit; talk brings poverty." Work is something you do, not just talk about. Throughout history, work has been man's chief activity, and the importance of labor is evident in our country.

There are three kinds of people who work:

Those who make things happen.

Those who watch things happen.

Those who have no idea what has happened!

Which category are you?

When it comes to pushing back fear, overcoming adverse circumstances, or building a business, being intentional and diligent will give you the power you need to succeed.

Many years ago, John Maxwell was in Albuquerque to speak at a pastor's conference, a few years before he launched his work as a leadership expert. A friend of mine was his "handler" while he was in town for the event. While having an evening meal, my pastor friend asked John, "What do you see down the road? You have built a thriving church; you are a respected author. What's next?"

Without hesitation, John said, "In the next five years I want to be known as America's Leadership Expert!"

Guess what? It happened.

Hope is the underlying principle for all change. People change because they have hope, and if people don't have hope, they will not change.

The Bible says, "Hope deferred make the heart sick, but a dream fulfilled is a tree of life," Proverbs 12:13 NLT.

Here is what happens when an individual experiences deferred hope. When a person loses their dream, the joy of living becomes replaced with the mere act of surviving or just getting by—the downward spiral from joy to subsistence, into depression, and ultimately despair. No one I know aspires to this.

My personal observation is that people who have lost hope, particularly in a business venture, didn't have a clear vision or dream that would sustain them in the lean times. Instead, they had wishes. Vision without action is only day-dreaming. Action without vision is just random activity. Both of these behaviors lead to nowhere happy. But when you combine work with a powerful dream or vision, you can change the world.

John Maxwell recommends six steps that will help you make the changes you need to live your life in a positive, impactful, God-honoring way. I believe his insights could be rooted in Philippians 4:8 (NLT) where the Apostle Paul says, "And now, dear brothers and sisters, one final thing. Fix your thoughts on what is true, and honorable, and right, and pure, and lovely, and admirable. Think about things that are excellent and worthy of praise."

Step # 1

When you begin to alter your thought life toward things in line with Philippians 4:8, you change your beliefs and when you change your beliefs you start to change your mind, your thoughts, your actions, and your outcomes.

Let me show you a little trick I have used in the various presentations at events all over the world. This is a simple tool that you can use to help manage your thoughts. Over the years, I have heard many sermons on this passage from 2 Corinthians 10:5 (AMP).

We are destroying sophisticated arguments and every exalted *and* proud thing that sets itself up against the [true] knowledge of God, and *we are* taking every thought *and* purpose captive to the obedience of Christ.

While it sounded great, I never really had anyone explain it to me. As I grew in my faith and in my understanding, I began to realize that there were strategies people could use to manage their thought life, to help them anticipate trouble and work their way around it. One of these strategies is the ATC model which I explained back in chapter three. I borrowed this model from Cognitive Behavioral Psychology, and I believe it is completely in line with scripture. Remember the model: A—Activating Event or Trigger. T—Thoughts which are automatic. C—Consequences.

Let's see how it works. I will begin a jingle, and you finish it, within 4 seconds, and try not use an Internet search to find the answer.

Winston tastes good like a _____.

Plop, plop, fizz, fizz,_____.

Most people under fifty-five give me a polite but blank stare on the first jingle, which goes, "Winston tastes good like a cigarette should." This song ran in various ads from 1955 to 1972 when it was pulled. In 1999, Advertising Age ranked it as the eighth-best jingle out of all radio and television ads aired in the 20th Century.

Ninety-five percent of people immediately remember the second example with a smile and usually sing it with me.

"Pop, pop, fizz, fizz, oh what a relief it is." Alka-Seltzer.

Both are examples of a trigger event, a thought process, that produced a feeling and behavior. If you can grasp that, you can experience some incredible changes in your personal life. Why? Because you are bringing your thought captive, that is, under your control.

Step # 2

When you adjust your beliefs, you shift your expectations. Belief is the knowledge and understanding we can do something that can be life-changing. It is the deep, gut feeling that what we undertake, we can accomplish. For the most part, all of us have the ability to look at something and know whether or not we can do it. So, in belief there is power. Our eyes and hearts are open, our opportunities open up, our visions become realities. You see, our faith system controls everything we do. If we believe we can, or we believe we cannot, we are correct.

Remember *The Little Engine That Could*? If you don't remember the story, you can find it through a quick Internet search.

Step # 3

When you adjust your expectations, you change your attitude. Most people get used to average; they get used to second best. Nelson Boswell says, "The first and most important step toward success in any endeavor is the expectation that we can succeed."

Step # 4

When you adjust your behaviors, you change your outcomes. Regarding fear, as you begin to change how you view it and take the action steps I've outlined, you will begin to push it back, make it more manageable, and use its energy to help propel you forward. The reason we need to make personal changes is that we cannot take others where we have not been willing to go ourselves.

Step # 5

When you change your behavior, you change your performance. Most people would rather live with old problems than new solutions. We'd rather be comfortable than correct. We would rather stay in a routine than make changes. Even when we know the changes are going to be better for us, we often don't make them because we feel uncomfortable or awkward about making that kind of change. Until we get courage and adjust to living with something that is not comfortable, for a season, we cannot get any better.

Step #6

When you change your performance, you change your life! It is easier to turn a failure into a success than an excuse into a possibility. A person can fail, turn around and learn from it, then convert it into success.

Many years ago, I attended the North Carolina Outward Bound School. Just before supper, our adult team leaders took us for a four-mile hike into an unfamiliar landscape. At least four times our leader stopped us at various intersections and had us look back and study each of those trail junctions. He had spent several years as a smoke jumper, so we listened. He said, "In life you are going to have failure, you are going to be in scary situations. Most people will run wildly away from trouble with no idea of where they are headed, but when you fail or are in a scary situation, you can always go back to a familiar trail junction to regain your bearings."

My friend, Dr. Jack Allen, says it this way: "When you make a mess, own the mess, confess the mess, and then clean it up."

This may sound harsh, but sometimes, for the truth to set you free, it has to hurt a little. A person who makes excuses for everything will never succeed at anything except blaming others and becoming a helpless, hapless victim. You and I have heard them. I used to be pretty good at making excuses. If you are looking for an excuse, any one will do.

Instead of being stuck in excuses, try to turn them into possibilities.

ABOUT THE AUTHOR

John Thurman is an author with more than thirty-five years experience in the people helping profession. He has served as an Army Chaplain, counselor, speaker, and international crisis response specialist.

John holds two Master degrees, a Masters of Divinity and a Master of Arts in Counseling.

He is known for his highly practical, uncomplicated communication style that is aimed at helping individuals live a more meaningful and resilient life.

He and his wife Angie live in New Mexico.

ENDNOTES

1   http://www.ourcatholicprayers.com/st-patricks-breastplate.html. Accessed September 12, 2016

2   Tito Philips, "7 Reasons Why Most Entrepreneurs Fail in Business," http://www.naijapreneur.com/why-entrepreneurs-fail/. Accessed December 2015.

3   http://www.motivation.com/quotes/62, Accessed November, 2016

4   Brett and Kate McKay, " "30 Days to a Better Man: Conquer Fear," http://www.artofmanliness.com/2009/06/28/30-days-to-a-better-man-day-29-conquer-a-fear/. Accessed February 2, 2016.

5   Theodore Roosevelt, "The Man in the Arena."

6   Leon Shane III, "Female Soldier Awarded Silver Star, Stars and Stripes. http://www.stripes.com/news/female-soldier-awarded-silver-star-1.34794. Accessed November 2014

7

8   http://www.biography.com/people/richard-branson-9224520. Accessed November 2014.

9   Danielle Beavers. (July 28, 2008). "Colbie Caillat: From 'American Idol' Reject To John Mayer Tourmate." MTV News. Retrieved March 2014

10   http://www.biography.com/people/buzz-aldrin-9179894. Accessed November 2014.

11   Annette Spence, "Convocation, Leonard Sweet Opens New Language Lines Between Cultural Divides," The Call, Vol. E 13, Number 5. http://holston.org/about/communications/the-call/volE13/num5/convocation/. Accessed July 2016.

12   Taylor Swift on Selena Gomez and Madonna: Singer Talks Giving Advice, Getting Inspirations, http://www.huffingtonpost.com/2013/05/25/taylor-swift-selena-gomez-madonna_n_3336565.html. Accessed August 2016

13   Joel Osteen, "8 Uplifting Sayings from Evangelical Christians, Newsmax, http://www.newsmax.com/FastFeatures/joel-osteen-inspirational-quotes-evangelical-christian/2015/05/03/id/641824/ Accessed June 2016.

14   Bruce Wilkerson, Quote, http://www.brainyquote.com/quotes/quotes/b/brucewilki633252.html. Accessed June 2013.

15   http://quotesgram.com/quote/bear-grylls-quotes/494677. Accessed November 16, 2016.

16   Marty Seligman and Steven F. Maier, "Failure to Escape Traumatic Shock," Journal of Experimental Psychology, Vol. 74, May (1967): 1. Accessed October 2015.

17   Kim J.J and Diamond D.M. "The Stressed Hippocampus, Synaptic Plasticity and Lost Memories. Natural Reviews – Neuroscience, Vol 3. June 2002, pp 453-461.

18   Darius Styl, "Understanding the Fear of Criticism: According to Napoleon Hill," Christian Rationality. Reason. Faith. Christ .Virtue. http://www.christianrationality.com/2016/08/08/understanding-the-fear-of-criticism-

according-to-napoleon-hill/ (Author's note – this is an interesting read!) Accessed August 2016.

19   Victor Parachin, "The Moon Keeps on Shining"…and Other Ways of Dealing with Criticism." Leadership with a Conscience, http://www. perdidomagazine.com/articles/moon-keeps-shining-and-other-ways-dealing-criticism. Accessed August 2015.

20   Dr. Seuss, http://www.quotationspage.com/quote/29739.html. Accessed August 2015.

21   Denis Waitley, http://www.forbes.com/sites/ ekaterinawalter/2013/12/30/30-powerful-quotes-on-failure/#2355292515d3

22   Angela Hughes, "Why Failure Could be the Best Thing That Ever Happened to You," Charisma Magazine. http://www.charismamag.com/life/ women/22227-why-failure-could-be-the-best-thing-that-ever-happened-to-you. Accessed August 2016.

23   Michael Jordan, "Famous Failures," Success Magazine. Nov 16, 2013. http://www.success.com/article/famous-failures. Accessed December 2013.

24   J.K.Rowling, "Rebounding from Failure," http://www.jkrowling.com/ en_US/#/timeline/rebounding-from-failure. Accessed May 2015.

25   Travis Bradberry, "8 Ways Smart People Use Failure to Their Advantage." Inc. Magazine, http://www.jkrowling.com/en_US/#/timeline/rebounding-from-failure. Accessed August 2016.

26   Julie Sprankles, "Stories of Survival: Female Celebs Who've Overcome Adversity, Published July 14, 2014. http://www.sheknows.com/entertainment/ articles/1027977/stories-of-survival-female-celebs-whove-overcome-adversity. Accessed September 2014.

27   Julie Zellinger, "7 Influential Women Who Failed Before They Succeeded," The Huffington Post, US Edition, Published July 24, 2013. http:// www.huffingtonpost.com/2013/07/24/7-women-who-failed-before-they-succeeded_n_3640835.html . Accessed October 2014.

28   Ibid.

29   L.R. Knost, Quotes, http://www.goodreads.com/author/ quotes/5116439.L_R_Knost. Accessed May 2016.

30   Marina Krakovsky, "The Effort Effect," Stanford Alumni, Published January 2010. http://alumni.stanford.edu/get/page/magazine/article/?article_ id=32124. Accessed April 2013.

31   http://www.drmichellemazur.com/2013/02/5-of-the-smartest-things-ever-said-about-public-speaking.html. Accessed September 2016.

32   http://likesuccess.com/1392860. Accessed May 2016.

33   Holly Gerth, You're Going to Be Okay: Encouraging Truth Your Heart Needs to Hear, Especially on the Hard Days,(Grand Rapids: Michigan, Fleming H. Revell Company, 2014.

34   Leneka, http://psychologyforphotographers.com/about-the-author. Accessed August 2016.

35   James Clear, "Lessons on Sharing Your Gifts With the World From Someone Who Didn't," http://jamesclear.com/vivian-maier. Accessed November 2015.

36   Ibid.
37   http://www.christianitytoday.com/biblestudies/bible-answers/spirituallife/christianview.html. Accessed August,, 2016.
38   http://www.brainyquote.com/quotes/topics/topic_change.html Accessed October 2016.
39   http://fivepatterns.com/overview.php. Accessed August 2015.
40   http://www.brainyquote.com/quotes/quotes/j/joycemeyer565183.html. Accessed March 2015.
41   Ibid.
42   Joan Horner, Gems from Joan, Published 2011.

www.ingramcontent.com/pod-product-compliance
Lightning Source LLC
LaVergne TN
LVHW051250080426
835513LV00016B/1843